WHAT SMALL GROUP LEA
MEMBERS ARE SAYING A
Experiencing Christ Togeth...

My group was formed four years ago of very new believers. EXPERIENCING CHRIST TOGETHER has helped form bonds, and we have fallen in love with Christ. We have had many trials, but we have learned to lean on the body of Christ to carry us through the difficult times. I know our lives are richer than ever.

—Leader

The EXPERIENCING CHRIST TOGETHER series has motivated me more than any other Bible study that I have ever been to. This Bible study gets to the heart of the matter—my character in Christ—and that has created action on my part.

—Leader

I love the fact that Jesus' life shows us how to live.

—Member

This series is an "awakening." Jesus has become a very personal friend.

—Leader

This series is definitely a must-do as the foundation for a healthy, maturing small group!

—Leader

EXPERIENCING CHRIST TOGETHER is a safe place to learn about the living Jesus and how he wants to lead us and love us.

—Member

EXPERIENCING CHRIST TOGETHER ties the heart and the mind together. The Bible knowledge grows the mind and the life application grows the heart and transforms the soul.

—Member

Other Studies in the EXPERIENCING CHRIST TOGETHER Series

Beginning in Christ Together (Life of Jesus)

Connecting in Christ Together (Fellowship)

Growing in Christ Together (Discipleship)

Sharing Christ Together (Evangelism)

Surrendering to Christ Together (Worship)

Studies in the DOING LIFE TOGETHER Series

Beginning Life Together (God's Purpose for Your Life)

Connecting with God's Family (Fellowship)

Growing to Be Like Christ (Discipleship)

Developing Your SHAPE to Serve Others (Ministry)

Sharing Your Life Mission Every Day (Evangelism)

Surrendering Your Life to God's Pleasure (Worship)

experiencing
CHRIST
together

SERVING LIKE CHRIST TOGETHER

six sessions on
Ministry

written by
BRETT and DEE EASTMAN
TODD and DENISE WENDORFF
KAREN LEE-THORP

ZONDERVAN™

GRAND RAPIDS, MICHIGAN 49530 USA

We want to hear from you. Please send your comments about this book to us in care of zreview@zondervan.com. Thank you.

ZONDERVAN™

Serving Like Christ Together
Copyright © 2005 by Brett and Deanna Eastman, Todd and Denise Wendorff, and Karen Lee-Thorp

Requests for information should be addressed to:
Zondervan, *Grand Rapids, Michigan 49530*

ISBN 0-310-24984-8

Interior icons by Tom Clark

Interior design by Beth Shagene & Michelle Espinoza

Printed in the United States of America

05 06 07 08 09 10 11 /❖ DCI/ 10 9 8 7 6 5 4 3 2

CONTENTS

EXPERIENCING CHRIST TOGETHER

EXPERIENCING CHRIST TOGETHER: LIVING WITH PURPOSE IN COMMUNITY will take you face to face with Jesus himself. In addition to being the Son of God and Savior of the world, Jesus holds the greatest wisdom and understands the purposes for which God formed you. He knows what it takes to build authentic relationships, to know God more intensely, to grow spiritually, and ultimately to make a difference in the world. EXPERIENCING CHRIST TOGETHER offers you a chance to do what Jesus' first followers did: spend time with him, listen to what he said, watch what he did, and pattern your life after his.

Jesus lived every moment following God's purpose for his life. In this study you will experience firsthand how he did this and how you can do it too. Yet if you're anything like us, knowing what God wants for you is one thing, but doing it is something else. That's why you'll follow Jesus' plan of doing life not alone but together. As you follow in his footsteps, you'll find his pathway more exciting than anything you've imagined.

Book 1 in this series (*Beginning in Christ Together*) explores the person of Jesus Christ. Each of the subsequent five studies looks through Jesus' eyes at one of God's five biblical purposes for his people (fellowship, discipleship, service, evangelism, and worship). For example, *Serving Like Christ Together* deals with ministry, or service. Book 1 is about grace: what Christ has done for us. The other books are about how we live in response to grace.

Even if you've done another LIFE TOGETHER study, you'll be amazed at how Jesus can take you to places of faith you've never been before. The joy of life in him is far beyond a life you could design on your own. If you do all six study guides in this series, you'll spend one astonishing year with Jesus Christ.

Thinking Like a Servant

The philosopher Friedrich Nietzsche complained that Christianity was a religion for slaves. He thought attitudes like compassion, humility, and sacrifice were for wimps. The world, he believed, would be better off with a religion for masters. Many people agree with him. Power, self-confidence, success—those seem like qualities worth cultivating.

Jesus saw things very differently. He thought pride, self-focus, and indifference to others' needs were the real slavery. He understood what happened to a person who spent a lifetime developing such heart-shrinking habits. So he guided his disciples toward habits that would lead naturally to freehearted, wholehearted service.

Serving Like Christ Together explores six qualities of a servant's heart that Jesus highly valued. In addition to Bible study, you'll have practical opportunities to serve one another and those outside your group. You'll support one another in personal growth and cap your study with a service project of your choice that you can do together. If you want to deepen the intimacy in your group, there's nothing better you can do than serve Christ together.

Service shouldn't be something we force ourselves to do because we'll be punished if we don't. It should flow from a heart formed as Christ's is, by a passion for something greater than ourselves. Nietzsche thought that was slave thinking. What do *you* believe is the real route to freedom?

Outline of Each Session

Most people want to live healthy, balanced spiritual lives, but few achieve this alone. And most small groups struggle to balance all of God's purposes in their meetings. Groups tend to overemphasize one of the five purposes, perhaps fellowship or discipleship. Rarely is there a healthy balance that includes evangelism, ministry, and worship. That's why we've included all of these elements in this study so you can live a healthy, balanced spiritual life over time.

A typical group session will include the following:

 CONNECTING WITH GOD'S FAMILY (FELLOWSHIP). The foundation for spiritual growth is an intimate connection with God and his family. A few people who really know you and who earn your trust provide a place to experience the life Jesus invites you to live. This section of each session offers you two options. You can get to know your whole group by using the icebreaker question (always question 1), or you can check in with one or two group members—your spiritual partner(s)—for a deeper connection and encouragement in your spiritual journey.

DVD TEACHING SEGMENT. A DVD companion to this study guide is available. For each study session, a teacher discusses the topic, ordinary Christians talk about the personal experience of the topic, a scholar gives background on the Bible passage, and a leadership coach gives tips to the group leader. The DVD contains worship helps and other features as well. If you are using the DVD, you will view the teaching segment after your Connecting discussion and before your Bible study (the Growing section). At the end of each session in this study guide you will find space for your notes on the teaching segment. To view a sample of the DVD, log on to www.lifetogether.com/ExperiencingChristTogether.

GROWING TO BE LIKE CHRIST (DISCIPLESHIP). Here is where you come face to face with Christ. In a core Bible passage you'll see Jesus in action, teaching or demonstrating some aspect of how he wants you to live. The focus won't be on accumulating information but on how Jesus' words and actions relate to what you say and do. We want to help you apply the Scriptures practically, creatively, and from your heart as well as your head. At the end of the day, allowing the timeless truths from God's Word to transform our lives in Christ is our greatest aim.

FOR DEEPER STUDY. If you want to dig deeper into more Bible passages about the topic at hand, we've provided additional passages and questions. Your group may choose to do study homework ahead of each meeting in order to cover more biblical material. Or you as an individual may choose to study the For Deeper Study passages on your own. If you prefer not to do study homework, the Growing section will provide you with plenty to discuss within the group. These options allow individuals or the whole group to go deeper in their study, while still accommodating those who can't do homework or are new to your group.

You can record your discoveries on the Reflections page at the end of each session. We encourage you to read some of your insights to a friend (spiritual partner) for accountability and support. Spiritual partners may check in each week over the phone, through email, or at the beginning of the group meeting.

DEVELOPING YOUR GIFTS TO SERVE OTHERS (MINISTRY). Jesus trained his disciples to discover and develop their gifts to serve others. God has designed you uniquely to serve him in a way no other person can. This section will help you discover and use your God-given design. It will also encourage your group to discover your unique design as a community. Throughout this study, you'll put into practice what you've learned in the Bible study by taking a step to serve others. These simple steps will take your group on a faith journey that could change your lives forever.

 SURRENDERING YOUR LIFE FOR GOD'S PLEASURE (WORSHIP). God is most pleased by a heart that is fully his. Each group session will give you a chance to surrender your heart to God in prayer and worship. You may read a psalm together, share a page in your journal, or use one of the songs on the DVD to open or close your meeting. (Additional music is available on the LIFE TOGETHER Worship DVD/CD series, produced by Maranatha!) If you've never prayed aloud in a group before, no one will put pressure on you. Instead, you'll experience the support of others who are praying for you. This time will knit your hearts in community and help you surrender all your hurts and dreams into the hands of the One who knows you best.

STUDY NOTES. This section provides background notes on the Bible passage(s) you examine in the Growing section. You may want to refer to these notes during your group meeting or as a reference for those doing additional study.

REFLECTIONS. At the end of each session is a blank page on which you can write your insights from your personal time with God. Whether you do deeper Bible study, read through the Gospels, meditate on a few verses, or simply write out your prayers, you'll benefit from writing down what you discover. You may want to pick up a blank journal or notepad after you fill in these pages.

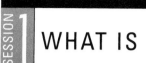

WHAT IS SUCCESS?

The Fourth of July in a California beach city meant hundreds of celebrating visitors. By the next morning, trash always littered the streets. Evan decided that it would be great for his group to serve the town by picking up trash. Then other groups in his church heard the idea and decided to join in. On the fifth of July, almost a hundred people were out on the beach and wandering through town, picking up and bagging trash. They had a great day serving together. It wasn't the most glorious job, but the community had a need and God's servants responded.

From that day on, the city felt that Evan's church really cared. The city began to go to that church for a variety of needs and asked the church to host special events. All of this was possible because when there was a need, people responded.

CONNECTING WITH GOD'S FAMILY   20 min.

Service is often unglamorous, like picking up trash that others have left. For some of us, our natural reaction is that such jobs are beneath us. For others of us, no act of service is beneath us because we've acquired Jesus' servant heart. In each session of this study, you're going to look at a different aspect of a servant heart. You'll begin with a servant's attitude toward success and importance.

1. In a sentence or two, describe someone you think is successful. What makes that person successful in your eyes? (Please don't tell a long story here or you'll cut into your Bible study time.)

2. Whether your group is brand new or ongoing, it's always important to reflect on and review your values together. On pages 74–75 is a sample agreement with the values we've found most useful in sustaining healthy, balanced groups. We recommend that you choose one or two values—ones you haven't previously focused on or have room to grow in—to emphasize during this study. Choose ones that will take your group to the next stage of intimacy and spiritual health.

A great one for this study would be shared ownership. Make it your goal to find a way for each group member to serve the group in some way: hosting, bringing refreshments, planning a group service project, leading the worship, calling members who miss a meeting, and so on. Pages 77–79 contain some ideas, as does session 3.

We also recommend that you rotate host homes on a regular basis and let the hosts lead the meeting. This helps to develop every member's ability to shepherd a few people in a safe environment. Even Jesus gave others the opportunity to serve alongside him (Mark 6:30–44). Session 2 will explain how to set up a rotating schedule.

GROWING TO BE LIKE CHRIST   25 min.

Our culture places a high value on individual success and personal fulfillment. Success is often measured in money—the more money you make, the more successful you are. Business, politics, professions, and sports are good routes to success. You can be successful as an artist if you make enough money at it. Success is also measured in fame—how many people know about you and what you've done.

Another strand of our culture says it's not enough to make money—you also need to feel personally fulfilled in what you do. Being truly successful is getting rich and feeling fulfilled at the same time.

We also have standards for judging the success of parents (raise smart, moral Christian kids who go on to have successful careers and families) and churches (grow larger congregations, buildings, and budgets). A society is successful if crime and war don't threaten it, and if the standard of living (measured in money) is growing.

Jesus' disciples had ideas about success too, and they thought following Jesus would lead there. But Jesus had his own ideas.

3. Read Mark 10:35–45. On page 18, read the study note for "sit at your right . . . left." What was James and John's picture of success?

4. How did politically successful people typically behave, according to Jesus (verse 42)?

5. How is this like or unlike the way successful people usually act today?

6. In what ways is Jesus' route to greatness different (verses 43–45)?

7. What would it look like for you to pursue that route to greatness?

8. What costs would that involve? Think about your career, your family relationships, your time and money.

What would be the benefits?

FOR DEEPER STUDY

How are God's values and the world's values in conflict, according to Luke 16:13–15? How do you think a person can tell if he or she is serving money rather than God?

Why do you think humility is so important to God (Luke 14:11; James 4:6)?

Why did Jesus oppose the human tendency to put spiritual leaders on pedestals (Matthew 23:1–12)?

What attitudes did Paul urge slaves to have in Ephesians 6:5–8? How did Paul tell masters to behave in Ephesians 6:9? Why did Paul urge Philemon to free his slave Onesimus in Philemon 8–19? Why do you suppose Paul didn't tell all masters to free their slaves? How do you think Paul's words to masters and slaves are relevant in today's workplace?

DEVELOPING YOUR GIFTS FOR SERVICE 25 min.

Jesus emphasizes humility and sacrifice. Humility doesn't mean thinking badly of yourself; it means thinking of yourself less and others more. Sacrifice means taking action that costs you something for the sake of others.

Humility makes no sense unless you believe a good God is taking care of your needs. Likewise, sacrifice makes sense only if the goal outweighs the cost.

9. In what ways do you expect others to serve you? Think broadly: restaurant workers, store clerks, family members, work colleagues, office janitors, others.

10. How do you typically treat these persons who serve you? In what ways do you "lord it over them" (Mark 10:42)? In what ways do you show respect for them?

11. In what current situation could you treat someone else with humble service?

12. Humility and sacrifice become natural as you learn to see life through Jesus' eyes. On page 16 offers are several options that will help you to see through his eyes. If you're new in your faith, feel free to select one of the simpler options. If you've been walking with God for some time, we encourage you to stretch yourself.

☐ *Prayer.* Ask God to show you ways in which others serve you. When you notice them, remember to say thank you.

☐ *Prayer.* Ask God to show you opportunities to serve others during the week. Commit to praying for this insight throughout this study, both with your group and on your own. Ask him to help you see and respond to people as he would.

☐ *Action.* When you see an opportunity to serve, act on it! Consciously cultivate this habit for the next six weeks.

☐ *Action.* Invite someone to join this group! Who do you know who would benefit from a group like this?

☐ *Gospel Reading.* Read through the gospel of Matthew. On pages 87–88 is a reading plan. We recommend that you jot down your thoughts on the Reflections page or in a journal.

☐ *Meditation.* If you've read Matthew before, try meditation as a way of internalizing God's Word more deeply. Copy a portion of each week's Bible study passage onto a card, and tape it somewhere in your line of sight, such as on your car's dashboard or the kitchen table. Think about it when you sit at red lights, or while you're eating a meal. What is God saying to you, here and now, through these words? Alternative passages for meditation are suggested on the Reflections page at the end of each session. You may use that page to write your responses to your meditation verses.

13. Pair up with someone in your group. This person will be your "spiritual partner." If you've done another study in this series, you may keep the same partner or rotate to someone else.

On pages 20–21 is a Personal Health Plan, a chart to help you track your spiritual progress. In the box that says, "WHO are you connecting with spiritually?" write your partner's name. In the box that says, "WHAT is your next step for growth?" write the step you chose in question 12.

Tell your partner what step you chose. When you check in with your partner each week, this chart will provide a place to record his or her progress as well as your own.

If you have more than one partner, an additional health plan is on pages 82–83 in the Appendix. Also, on pages 84–85 you'll find a completed health plan filled in as an example.

SURRENDERING YOUR LIFE FOR GOD'S PLEASURE   15-30 min.

14. When we truly see Jesus as the one who gave his life for us, worship naturally follows. Take some time to respond to Jesus, who leads by serving. Here are two ideas:

   ☐ Philippians 2:6–11 is probably an early Christian worship song. You can use it for your own worship. Read 2:3–11 aloud. One approach is to let three or more readers take turns each reading a verse. Or let half the group read the odd-numbered verses and the other half read the even-numbered verses. Afterward, allow some open time for the group to add spontaneous words of praise.

   ☐ Use a song from the DVD, the LIFE TOGETHER Worship DVD/CD series, or a CD of your choice to worship God with music.

15. Gather into circles of three or four people so that everyone has time to share and pray. Ask one person to volunteer to write down prayer requests in the Prayer and Praise Report on page 22. Then allow everyone to answer this question: "How can we pray for you this week?" Take some time to pray for these requests.

STUDY NOTES

Jesus' disciples had been with him for three years. They were convinced he was the Messiah: the warrior-king who would overthrow the Romans and establish God's kingdom on earth. Through teaching and miracles he had displayed messianic authority. Some of his teaching about God's kingdom puzzled his disciples, but they were sure they knew what a kingdom was.

Now Jesus was on his way to Jerusalem, where his disciples expected him to march into the temple, claim the title of Messiah, and begin the uprising. They were so sure victory was imminent that they began angling for their rank in the kingdom.

James and John (Mark 10:35). Brothers who worked in their father's fishing business until Jesus called them to become disciples (1:19–20). They were nicknamed "Sons of Thunder" (3:17), probably a reference to their temperament.

Sit at your right . . . left (10:37). Jesus had already promised that his disciples would sit on thrones next to him to judge the tribes of Israel (Matthew 19:28). But James and John's timing and motivation were off: they wouldn't get these thrones until they were in paradise, after lives of service to Christ. Their lives of sacrifice would be their badges of honor as they sat on those glorious thrones. Also, the seats on the King's right and left were the seats of highest honor. James and John were asking for status above the other disciples.

Cup . . . baptism (10:38). The agony Jesus would endure for the world's sake. James and John weren't destined for agony as intense as Jesus', but James was going to die for his faith (Acts 12:2) and John would end his life in exile on an island (Revelation 1:9). Though God gives us salvation by grace, we inherit the full blessings of the kingdom if we're willing to suffer whatever is necessary in God's service.

Slave (10:44). *Doulos* in Greek. Paul called himself Christ's *doulos* (Romans 1:1). We don't own ourselves; our Master bought us with his blood (1 Corinthians 6:19–20). But here Jesus talks about thinking of ourselves not merely as his slaves, but as one another's. Only God—not another human being—can own us. But Jesus uses this graphic word to impress on us an attitude of selfless service to one another.

Ransom (10:45). The Greek *lytron* literally meant the price of one's release. A slave could be bought. The one making the payment owned the slave. Jesus' own life is payment of our release from slavery to sin and eternal separation from God.

Our culture highly prizes liberty. We celebrate our freedom to do what we want. But the biblical writers believed that nobody is a completely free agent. If we don't choose to serve God, our choices quickly entangle us in slavery to harmful habits (Luke 16:13; Romans 6:15–23).

PERSONAL HEALTH PLAN

This worksheet could become your single most important feature in this study. On it you can record your personal priorities before the Father. It will help you live a healthy spiritual life, balancing all five of God's purposes.

PURPOSE	PLAN
CONNECT	WHO are you connecting with spiritually?
GROW	WHAT is your next step for growth?
DEVELOP	WHERE are you serving?
SHARE	WHEN are you shepherding another in Christ?
SURRENDER	HOW are you surrendering your heart?

If you have more than one partner, another Personal Health Plan can be found in the Appendix or downloaded in a larger format at www.lifeto-gether.com/healthplan. A Sample Health Plan is also in the Appendix.

DATE	MY PROGRESS	PARTNER'S PROGRESS

PRAYER AND PRAISE REPORT

Briefly share your prayer requests with the large group, making notations below. Then gather in smaller groups of two to four to pray for each other.

Date: _____

Prayer Requests

_____
_____
_____
_____
_____
_____
_____
_____
_____
_____

Praise Report

_____
_____
_____
_____
_____
_____
_____
_____
_____
_____
_____

REFLECTIONS

Use this page to write out your prayers, your thoughts about your daily Bible reading, or your meditations on a verse from the passage you have already studied. Below are some suggested verses for meditation. The Bible Reading Plan is on pages 87–88.

For Meditation: Mark 10:45 or 10:42–45

For Gospel Reading:

- What do I *learn* from the life of Christ (his identity, personality, priorities)?

- How does he want me to *live* differently?

_____

_____

_____

_____

_____

_____

_____

_____

_____

_____

_____

_____

_____

_____

_____

_____

_____

_____

_____

DVD NOTES

If you are watching the accompanying *Serving Like Christ Together* DVD, write down what you sense God saying to you through the speaker. (If you'd like to hear a sample of the DVD teaching segment, go to www.lifetogether.com/ExperiencingChristTogether.)

_____

_____

_____

_____

_____

_____

_____

_____

_____

_____

_____

_____

_____

_____

_____

_____

_____

_____

_____

_____

_____

_____

_____

SERVING CHRIST IN OTHERS

Steve had two first-row tickets to the seventh game of the World Series. After much thought, he gave them to Andrew. Andrew was eleven years old and had a brain stem tumor that, according to his doctors, would take his life within six months. The Make-a-Wish Foundation had put Steve in touch with Andrew's father, who took Andrew to the game.

Andrew's father called Steve after the game. With tears he said it was the best day of his son's life. Steve realized that going to the game himself would never have given him the joy he felt because he gave the tickets away. He hopes this will be the first of many acts of generosity in his future.

Steve displayed an aspect of a servant's heart: serving a person in need as we would serve Christ. As you saw in session 1, the heart attitude fuels the action.

CONNECTING WITH GOD'S FAMILY   10 min.

You may begin this session by connecting with your whole group about things that have happened in your lives since your last meeting (question 1). Or you may begin by letting spiritual partners check in to encourage each other (question 2).

1. One thing that helps our servant hearts grow is noticing when others serve us. How did someone serve you in the past week?

    Or,

2. Check in with your spiritual partner(s), or with another partner if yours is absent. What is something you learned or gained from your personal time with God this week (prayer, Bible reading, and/or journaling)? Or, did you seize a chance to serve someone this week?

GROWING TO BE LIKE CHRIST   30 min.

Salvation is God's gift to us; we don't earn it. We are saved, forgiven for sin, and welcomed into God's family when we place our faith in Christ, who died for us. This is bedrock biblical truth.

Jesus knew this when he was training his disciples, even before he went to the cross. Yet when he taught them how to prepare for the day when they would stand before him in glory, he spoke sometimes about faith and sometimes about actions. Faith and action go hand in hand. Our service flows out of our commitment to Christ.

3. Read Matthew 25:31–46. What did the sheep "who are blessed by my Father" do while they awaited Christ's return in glory?

4. Why are these actions so important to the King (verse 40)?

5. What is the inheritance for those who obey the King in these ways (verses 31–34, 46)?

6. What destiny awaits those who fail to do these things (verses 41, 46)?

7. Jesus says whatever we do for the least of our fellow believers, we do for him (Matthew 25:40). How should this affect our attitude toward service?

8. How easy is it for you to see Christ in the poor, sick, or imprisoned and to serve them as you would serve him? Why do you think that's the case?

9. Suppose a person says, "I can't do the things Jesus lists in Matthew 25:35–36 because I don't have enough time." What solutions could address the time problem?

10. Suppose a person says, "I can't do the things Jesus lists because I don't have enough money." What could address the money problem?

11. What do you think helps a person develop the awareness that whatever he or she does, or doesn't do, for another believer is done to Christ?

FOR DEEPER STUDY

In Matthew 7:15–23, Jesus talks about the link between the faith of our hearts and the evidence in our behavior (fruit). What's the link? Why is it so important to have good fruit? At the same time, why isn't service (including even miracles) enough if we don't know Christ intimately?

How does James describe the link between faith and action in James 2:18–26? How does Jesus describe the link between intimacy with him and bearing fruit in John 15:1–16? Do you think these passages conflict with the idea that we are saved solely by grace through faith, apart from works? Why or why not?

DEVELOPING YOUR GIFTS FOR SERVICE   25 min.

It's often difficult to go out on our own to feed the hungry, host strangers, and visit people in prison. Jesus intended for communities of believers to do these things. One person doesn't have enough time, enough money, and enough gifts to meet these needs alone, but together we have everything it takes. Also, the best way to discover and develop how God has uniquely designed us to serve him is to start serving. Our gifts emerge and grow as we take action.

12. Begin planning a service project that you will do as a group within the next six weeks. It can be anything your group can do together to serve the needs of one or more persons outside your group. Feeding the hungry, providing water for the thirsty, inviting strangers to your home, clothing the poor, caring for the sick, or visiting prisoners—all these are good ideas. Your pastor or city hall may have ideas for outreach to the poor in

your area. One of you may know an elderly person who needs help with tasks around the home. In fact, one of you may already be caring for an aging parent or ill relative—how can your group share the burden? Who are the single mothers in your church? Brainstorm a list of ideas.

13. Now, which one or two group members are willing to coordinate this project and plan the details? The group leader shouldn't have to carry the load, and other group members need this chance to develop their leadership and organizational gifts. Two volunteers will be better than one, and more will be great!

14. "Rotating leaders" is one of the group values we highly recommend for your group. People need opportunities to experiment with ways in which God may have gifted them. If you have never led before, don't panic. Your main group leader will be available to coach you as you experiment. You may also rotate host homes as well, with the host of each meeting providing the refreshments as well as leading the discussion. (You may also rotate host homes without requiring hosts to lead the discussion.)

   The Small Group Calendar on page 76 is a tool for planning who will host and lead each meeting. Take a few minutes to plan hosts and leaders for your next three meetings.

   If you like, you may write one of these steps in "WHERE are you serving?" on your Personal Health Plan on page 20.

 SURRENDERING YOUR LIFE FOR GOD'S PLEASURE 15-30 min.

15. Team up with one or two people and share the one area of your life where you need God most or where God most wants to work. In James 5:16, James encourages you to confess to and pray for each other so that you may be healed.

16. Need an idea for worship? Have someone reread Matthew 25:31–32 aloud. Then take a minute of silence to picture this scene: Christ on his throne. Let this picture carry you into worship of Christ through prayer or song.

STUDY NOTES

Separate ... sheep from the goats (Matthew 25:32). Sheep and goats normally grazed together during the day, but at night the herdsman separated them.[1] Jesus portrays himself as the shepherd of all people. At the end of this age, Jesus will judge unbelievers and pseudo believers, separating them from his true followers (Revelation 20:11–15).

On his right (25:33). The right side represents a place of power and honor (1 Kings 2:19).

Lord, when did we ... (25:37)? Jesus' sheep are surprised that reward awaits their faithfulness. They did not serve others because they knew this was the only way to prevent being separated from their master. They did it because they had taken on their master's character, including his genuine heart to serve others.

These brothers of mine (25:40). Here Jesus focuses on treating fellow believers as we would treat Christ. Yet the full counsel of Scripture urges us to serve unbelievers in the same ways (Isaiah 58:6–7; Luke 6:27–36).

Eternal fire ... eternal punishment (25:41, 46). Jesus did not leave a person's eternal destiny to question. If you truly believe in him, you will naturally seek ways to serve him. If you serve Christ by serving others, your life will show the genuineness of your faith. If your inner motivation is only to care for yourself, that reveals a heart not surrendered to Christ. Such a person is subject to eternal separation from God and his disciples. God never intended people to go to hell. Yet because of their refusal to love him, a place of eternal separation and misery exists.

---

[1] D. A. Carson, "Matthew," *The Expositor's Bible Commentary, New Testament,* Frank E. Gaebelein, gen. ed., in Zondervan Reference Software, version 2.8 (Grand Rapids: Zondervan, 1998).

PRAYER AND PRAISE REPORT

Briefly share your prayer requests with the large group, making notations below. Then gather in smaller groups of two to four to pray for each other.

Date: _____

Prayer Requests

_____

_____

_____

_____

_____

_____

_____

_____

_____

Praise Report

_____

_____

_____

_____

_____

_____

_____

_____

_____

REFLECTIONS

Use this page to write out your prayers, your thoughts about your daily Bible reading, or your meditations on a verse from the passage you have already studied. Below are some suggested verses for meditation. The Bible Reading Plan is on pages 87–88.

For Meditation: Matthew 25:31–32 or 25:40

For Gospel Reading:

- What do I *learn* from the life of Christ (his identity, personality, priorities)?

- How does he want me to *live* differently?

_____

_____

_____

_____

_____

_____

_____

_____

_____

_____

_____

_____

_____

_____

_____

_____

_____

_____

DVD NOTES

If you are watching the accompanying *Serving Like Christ Together* DVD, write down what you sense God saying to you through the speaker. (If you'd like to hear a sample of the DVD teaching segment, go to www.lifetogether.com/ExperiencingChristTogether.)

COMPASSION

Ellen watched as her neighbor, Meg, dealt with a volatile marriage and then separation. With several children and no job, Meg's future was dim. Though on occasion Ellen intervened, she felt overwhelmed by the situation and was almost reluctant to serve Meg and her family.

Then a small group in Ellen's community decided to take Meg's family under their wing. Members brought meals. Others hired Meg's teenagers to babysit and often spent hours just talking to them as they dropped them off at home. There were many phone calls to include Meg's children in family events and opportunities that would be fun for the kids. Group members made themselves available to talk to the kids and encourage them as they faced life without their father.

It was humbling for Ellen to see this group take action beyond what she was willing to do. Being involved in the day-in-day-out drama sometimes numbed Ellen's servant heart, so it was enormously helpful to have others with whom to share this important work.

CONNECTING WITH GOD'S FAMILY   10 min.

As before, you may begin by checking in as a whole group (question 1) or with spiritual partners one-on-one (question 2).

1. What needs of people have you noticed in the past week—either in the news or someone you know personally?

Or,

2. Sit with your spiritual partner. What is happening with the spiritual step you wrote in your health plan?

GROWING TO BE LIKE CHRIST

Compassion is the ability to feel or see another person's need, along with the decision to address that need through action. Jesus had both strong feelings and a firm commitment to act. He trained his disciples to show the same compassion to others. We cannot truly serve out of our giftedness without Jesus' kind of compassion.

3. Read Mark 6:30–44. The apostles have just returned from their first ministry trip on their own, without Jesus with them. How does Jesus care for their needs in verses 30–32?

4. But then other people with needs turn up. What is it about them that moves Jesus to compassion (verse 34)? How would you put this in your own words?

5. What does it take to see people through Jesus' eyes so that we notice when they're like sheep without shepherds?

6. What compassionate things does Jesus do for these people? What needs does he address?

7. The disciples have less compassion for the crowd. What factors limit their commitment to serve the crowd's needs (verses 35–37)?

8. Today we use the term "compassion fatigue" to describe the tendency to become numb to others' needs when we feel overwhelmed by them. Our televisions broadcast endless images of suffering in one part of the globe after another: a famine here, a war there, an injustice, a disease. Charitable organizations deluge us with mail. Our churches offer long lists of opportunities to serve; our family and friends also have needs.

Do you ever feel compassion fatigue? If so, how do you respond? If not, what do you think protects you from it?

9. How does Jesus respond to the disciples' compassion fatigue (verses 37–41)?

10. Read the study note for "ate and were satisfied" on page 39. How should Jesus' ability to provide a banquet with a few loaves and fish affect the way we approach service to others and concern for our own needs?

11. In what areas of your life is Jesus saying each of the following things?

"Come with me . . . to a quiet place and get some rest."

"You give them something to eat. [I will multiply your resources.]"

FOR DEEPER STUDY

How did Jesus respond with compassion in Matthew 9:36–38? Why did he respond that way? Who are the sheep without shepherds around you? What can you do for them?

Compare John's account of feeding the crowd (John 6:1–13) to Mark's. What additional insights do you get about Jesus and his mission?

Read Exodus 16:1–26. How do Jesus' actions echo this story?

DEVELOPING YOUR GIFTS FOR SERVICE   20 min.

12. Let those who are coordinating your service project update the group on their plans and any help they need.

13. Every Christian community needs a balance of serving one another's needs (as Jesus cared for his exhausted disciples) and the needs of others outside the group. How can you serve your group? Why not team up with another member to serve your group in one of the following areas?

☐ **Connect.** Coordinate plans for child care during group meetings.

☐ **Connect.** Plan a group social time at least four times a year.

☐ **Connect.** Notice a struggle in someone's life and respond with an encouraging note and/or practical help.

- [ ] ☐ **Grow.** Take your turn at leading your group meeting.
- [ ] ☐ **Grow.** If you're the leader, help someone else learn how to lead part or all of the meeting.
- [ ] ☐ **Share.** Coordinate a group missions project, such as supporting a missionary or doing an act of service for someone who doesn't go to church.
- [ ] ☐ **Surrender.** Come up with creative ideas for the group's worship time.
- [ ] ☐ **Surrender.** Manage the group's Prayer and Praise Report.

In your Personal Health Plan on page 20, under "WHERE are you serving?" write the step you're going to take.

SURRENDERING YOUR LIFE FOR GOD'S PLEASURE 15–30 min.

Surrendering our hearts to God isn't easy or even natural. But once we take that area of sin, temptation, disappointment, anxiety, sadness, anger, whatever, and bring it before the Father—first in private and then in community—our lives fall securely into the Father's arms.

14. Take a moment of quiet reflection and write on the Reflections page in this session. Simply finish this sentence: "Father, I need your help today with . . ."

    If time allows and you are willing, share what you wrote with your spiritual partner, friend, or spouse. Take a risk, and let someone treat you with compassion.

STUDY NOTES

Get some rest (Mark 6:31). Jesus modeled balance. He took time for rest and reflection. In Matthew 26:11 he said, "The poor you will always have with you." We will never fully meet the needs of hurting people, so we need to balance ministry with other priorities. Rest and reflection are priorities that keep us sharp to care for people.

Compassion (6:34). The Greek word *splagchnizomai* means to be moved from the gut. Deep feelings of concern for others come from within. They move us to do something, not just feel something. Jesus both felt and acted on deep feelings of compassion. Even more than multiplying the loaves, perhaps Jesus' greatest miracle in this passage was getting the disciples to feel compassion for the crowd.

Shepherd (6:34). Leaders were often compared to shepherds in the Old Testament (Ezekiel 34:11–16, 23–31). Jesus is the true Shepherd of Israel (Psalm 23:1).

Ate and were satisfied (6:42). The feeding of the five thousand recalls God's miraculous provision of food for the Israelites in the desert after they left Egypt. God provided a resin-like food called manna six days a week (Exodus 16), and when the people grumbled that they were sick of manna, God provided meat (Numbers 11). Moses complained to God, "Would they have enough if flocks and herds were slaughtered for them? Would they have enough if all the fish in the sea were caught for them?" (Numbers 11:22). But Jesus provided more than enough at his miraculous meal. The prophet Elisha fed a hundred men, saying that the Lord had promised, "They will eat and have some left over" (2 Kings 4:43). Mark wants us to know that Jesus is greater than Moses and Elisha. Jesus provides the messianic banquet promised in Isaiah 25:6–9 and echoed in the Lord's Supper (Mark 14:17–25).

PRAYER AND PRAISE REPORT

Briefly share your prayer requests with the large group, making notations below. Then gather in smaller groups of two to four to pray for each other.

Date: _____

Prayer Requests

_____

_____

_____

_____

_____

_____

_____

_____

_____

_____

Praise Report

_____

_____

_____

_____

_____

_____

_____

_____

_____

_____

REFLECTIONS

Use this page to write out your prayers, your thoughts about your daily Bible reading, or your meditations on a verse from the passage you have already studied. Below are some suggested verses for meditation. The Bible Reading Plan is on pages 87–88.

For Meditation: Mark 6:34 or 6:39–43

For Gospel Reading:

- What do I *learn* from the life of Christ (his identity, personality, priorities)?

- How does he want me to *live* differently?

_____

_____

_____

_____

_____

_____

_____

_____

_____

_____

_____

_____

_____

_____

_____

_____

_____

_____

DVD NOTES

If you are watching the accompanying *Serving Like Christ Together* DVD, write down what you sense God saying to you through the speaker. (If you'd like to hear a sample of the DVD teaching segment, go to www.lifeto-gether.com/ExperiencingChristTogether.)

_____

_____

_____

_____

_____

_____

_____

_____

_____

_____

_____

_____

_____

_____

_____

_____

_____

_____

_____

_____

_____

_____

_____

_____

_____

_____

THE HOLY SPIRIT

Susan was excited! "I am feeling the Holy Spirit helping me do things in my day-to-day life that I never would have done before!" she said. She had talked to a homeless man about Jesus, and her group gave him food. She talked to her mom about what she was learning in her small group. She even reached out to her neighbor when she saw the neighbor's husband arrested for domestic abuse. She listened to the neighbor talk and cry, and she told her that if she needed anything, to knock on her door.

Susan said, "God is doing these things through me! I can feel him helping me say the right words and take those steps to reach out. God is showing me need after need, and I am listening to him and doing what he tells me. I am so grateful and humbled that he would use me in these ways."

The Holy Spirit longs to work through us to serve others. Sometimes we feel him, and sometimes we don't, but he's always ready to come to our aid when service is needed.

CONNECTING WITH GOD'S FAMILY   10 min.

The area of a servant's heart that you'll look at this week is dependence on the Holy Spirit. You may begin by connecting either as a whole group or one-on-one with spiritual partners.

1. Which of the following best describes your life during the past week?

    ☐ Handling life just fine on my own
    ☐ Grateful for God's help in some key areas
    ☐ Teamed up with others to deal with a challenge
    ☐ Praying for guidance without a clear answer yet
    ☐ Drowning and desperate for help

    Or,

2. Meet with your spiritual partner(s). What has God been saying to you through your personal time with him and your opportunities to serve others?

GROWING TO BE LIKE CHRIST   30 min.

The evening before he was arrested, Jesus spent several hours preparing his disciples for life without his physical presence. He was going to his Father's house and leaving his followers on earth to continue his ministry. Of course, they still needed resources beyond their human means. For this the Father would send them the Holy Spirit.

Without the Holy Spirit none of us can serve as Jesus served. The Spirit is the power in a servant's heart.

3. Read John 14:15–27 and the study note for "Counselor." Why do we need the Holy Spirit to be our Counselor?

4. In practical terms, how does the Holy Spirit counsel, help, encourage, comfort, and intercede for us?

5. Jesus says, "If you love me, you will obey what I command" and "the Father . . . will give you another Counselor" (14:15–16). Jesus' command from a few paragraphs earlier is, "Love one another" (13:34). Therefore, what's the connection between actively loving one another and experiencing the Counselor's presence?

6. What does the Holy Spirit have to do with truth (14:16–17, 23–26; see also 16:12–15)?

7. The Spirit helps, strengthens, guides, and reveals truth to us. Why do we need this kind of aid for loving and serving others?

8. Have you experienced the Holy Spirit strengthening, guiding, and helping you serve others? If so, describe your experience. If not, why do you suppose that's the case?

9. Do you think we can always feel the Holy Spirit when he's helping us? Explain your view.

10. Jesus says he will show himself to those who obey his command to love others (14:21; see also 13:34). What, then, is the relationship between serving others and intimacy with Christ?

11. How can the Holy Spirit help us if we:

☐ Don't know the best way to serve someone?
☐ Want to treat someone with love but don't have loving feelings toward that person?
☐ Need to serve someone day after day for months?

FOR DEEPER STUDY

In John 7:37–39, Jesus speaks of the Holy Spirit as "streams of living water" flowing within us. What does he mean? How does that help us serve him?

What connections between the Holy Spirit and service does Paul draw in 1 Corinthians 12:1–11?

Have you experienced the Holy Spirit doing the things Jesus and Paul describe? If so, how? If not, what attitude and action does Jesus suggest in Luke 11:9–13?

DEVELOPING YOUR GIFTS FOR SERVICE   20 min.

The Holy Spirit longs to guide us in many areas—to know Christ more intimately, to love him more deeply, to serve him more fruitfully. However, when we seek wisdom from our Counselor, we are often most interested in guidance that will make our lives more pleasant. If I take this job, will it lead to financial success and personal fulfillment? Which potential marriage partner will make me happy?

The Holy Spirit is generally more focused on God's agenda. He wants us to ask questions such as, "Where is God at work around me? How can I contribute? What does God want done among the people in my life? What does God want to accomplish through me that will lead to no material gain, no applause from people, but only to God's glory?"

12. Provide each group member with a blank sheet of paper and ask them to write "Lord, how can I serve you?" at the top of it. Have someone pray briefly for the Holy Spirit to help, counsel, and teach you as his servants. Then allow five minutes of silence for members to write.

    You may write out your questions about service in general or an area of your life in particular. You may write about an opportunity to serve that's on your mind or about obstacles you face in serving God. You may write what you think the Spirit might be saying to you about service. Pray and write, or write a prayer.

13. Afterward, those who want to share what they wrote or what's on their mind may do so.

14. For homework, look for a service opportunity in which you get no reward other than the chance to serve someone. Pray for the Holy Spirit to open your eyes to opportunities.

SURRENDERING YOUR LIFE FOR GOD'S PLEASURE 15–30 min.

15. What is one current area of your life in which you would like the Holy Spirit's guidance and strength?

16. In your Prayer and Praise Report on page 50, write down everyone's responses to question 15. Then pray for the Holy Spirit's active presence in each person's life.

STUDY NOTES

Obey (John 14:15). Jesus didn't send the Holy Spirit simply to make our personal lives easier or more glamorous. The Spirit empowers us to express our love for Christ by loving/serving one another.

Counselor (14:16). The Greek word *parakletos* comes from two words: "to call" and "alongside." By the time of the New Testament it meant "counselor, intercessor, helper, one who encourages and comforts; in the NT it refers exclusively to the Holy Spirit and to Jesus Christ."[2]

Spirit of truth (14:17). The Holy Spirit also functions as a guide to what is true and real. He illumines God's Word so we can understand and apply it.

Show myself (14:21). One of the rewards of obedience is that God reveals himself to us more fully. We often feel far from God, but God loves to make himself real to those who serve him.

Peace I leave with you (14:27). The Holy Spirit is associated with peace. This world brings fear and uncertainty. The Holy Spirit

---

[2] "Parakletos," *Greek-English Reader's Lexicon,* in *The Zondervan Bible Study Library* CD-ROM, version 5.0 (Grand Rapids: Zondervan, 2003).

replaces these feelings with peace, a perfect confidence that God is in charge and knows what he is doing. In a Jewish context, "peace" means wholeness, completeness, God's best. The Holy Spirit is all of God's best for a believer. It is out of this wholeness and completeness that we are able to serve others in a healthy way.

PRAYER AND PRAISE REPORT

Briefly share your prayer requests with the large group, making notations below. Then gather in smaller groups of two to four to pray for each other.

Date: _____

Prayer Requests

_____

_____

_____

_____

_____

_____

_____

_____

_____

Praise Report

_____

_____

_____

_____

_____

_____

_____

_____

_____

_____

REFLECTIONS

Use this page to write out your prayers, your thoughts about your daily Bible reading, or your meditations on a verse from the passage you have already studied. Below are some suggested verses for meditation. The Bible Reading Plan is on pages 87–88.

For Meditation: John 14:15–17 or 14:27

For Gospel Reading:

- What do I *learn* from the life of Christ (his identity, personality, priorities)?

- How does he want me to *live* differently?

DVD NOTES

If you are watching the accompanying *Serving Like Christ Together* DVD, write down what you sense God saying to you through the speaker. (If you'd like to hear a sample of the DVD teaching segment, go to www.lifetogether.com/ExperiencingChristTogether.)

BONDSLAVES

Barbara's friend was leading a small group for moms, and the moms needed someone to watch their children. When Barbara's friend asked her to be the babysitter, Barbara cringed. The absolute last thing she wanted to do for three hours every Thursday morning was watch a group of toddlers. Her own children were older, and she was glad to be past the toddler stage. Sensing Barbara's reluctance, her friend played her trump card: "There's a woman on the block who has offered to watch the kids, but she's Buddhist and interested in being part of the group and exploring Christianity if we can find another sitter."

Barbara knew she was cornered but stalled for time. She avoided praying about it that night because she knew what God would say. She decided to say no to child care and to invite the Buddhist neighbor to church. But then she opened a book to the first chapter and read the first sentence: "It's not about you." God had nailed her. He wanted her to serve that group of moms and wasn't going to let her selfishness and fear get in the way.

Barbara doesn't know how her decision to serve that group of moms affected them. She may not find out until heaven. But she does know that God used that service project to touch her. She got so much satisfaction from loving those kids for six weeks that she began to seriously consider whether God was calling her to children's ministry. She said, "Maybe it *was* about me after all."

CONNECTING WITH GOD'S FAMILY   10 min.

How are your servant hearts doing? You may either connect as a whole group about your week (question 1) or let spiritual partners connect one-on-one (question 2).

1. Think back over the past week. Recall a time when you had the chance to serve and you either did or didn't follow through. Without going into details about what you did, share with the group how you felt. Proud? Frustrated? Joyful? Exploited? Grateful? Determined? Exhausted?

Or,

2. Sit with your spiritual partner(s). What has God been saying to you this week through your personal time with him and your opportunities to serve?

GROWING TO BE LIKE CHRIST   30 min.

In our culture we value few possessions more than personal freedom. The liberty to do as we choose, to set the course of our own lives—we regard these as fundamental rights. Who among us would willingly yield the freedom to read, write, and speak what we want or to worship as we please?

By contrast, the word "slavery" raises horrific images: Africans dragged from their homelands across the sea to do menial labor under miserable conditions. Rapes, beatings, families torn apart, daily humiliations.

It may naturally offend us to think of Jesus asking us to take on the attitude of a slave. Unfortunately, he does exactly that in the passage you're going to study. Many translations soften the blow by rendering the offensive word as "servant," but as you can see in the study note on page 58, he's talking about a bondslave who isn't free to quit and go to work for a different master. Jesus goes out of his way to shock his disciples into thinking more deeply about what it means to dedicate their lives to him.

3. Read Luke 17:7–10. How would you describe the attitudes toward ourselves and God that Jesus encourages in this passage?

4. What potential problems or abuses might this passage lead to?

5. Read John 8:31–47. How does Jesus describe the life of someone who wants to live free from God as Master?

6. So we have a choice between slavery to God and slavery to sin! Why are we ultimately not free when we walk away from God's agenda?

7. What do you think Jesus means when he says, "The truth will set you free" (John 8:32)?

8. Jesus calls the Devil "a liar and the father of lies" (John 8:44). What's the connection between lies and sin?

9. What are some of the lies the Devil tells us about serving God as our Master?

10. Many people are understandably leery of a God who expects them to place his agenda ahead of their own at all times. The slavemaster who cares deeply about his slave and looks out for his slave's best interests is rare, to say the least. Why should we trust God?

11. What are the implications of Luke 17:7–10 in your relationships with the Lord and other people?

FOR DEEPER STUDY

What motivations for thinking of yourself as God's slave does Paul give in Romans 6:15–23? Is there anything in this passage that you don't understand?

How does Mary demonstrate the attitude of a slave/servant of God in Luke 1:26–38?

How does Samuel demonstrate a slave/servant's attitude in 1 Samuel 3:1–21?

How does Paul demonstrate the same attitude in 1 Corinthians 9:19–23?

What do you think about the idea that you belong to God, that he bought you and you don't belong to yourself? Which parts of you agree with that? Which parts of you resist the idea, and why?

DEVELOPING YOUR GIFTS FOR SERVICE   20 min.

12. In most groups, families, or workplaces, there are usually some persons who think of their duties ahead of their rights—who defer to others, who listen, who serve. Also, there are often some who think of their rights ahead of their duties—who strive to get their way, who are happy to let others carry the heaviest load, and who may even take advantage of others. How do you think the more service-minded members of a group should deal with a situation like this?

13. What are some practical needs of others that you could help to meet this week?

14. Let those who are planning your service project give an update to the group.

SURRENDERING YOUR LIFE FOR GOD'S PLEASURE   15–30 min.

Taking on the attitude of God's bondslave is a significant act of surrender. It makes sense only if you love and trust God as your Master.

15. Gather in a smaller circle of three or four people. What is one area of your life that you need to entrust to God? How easy is it for you to trust God in this area? Pray for each other about the areas you have shared.

STUDY NOTES

Servant (Luke 17:7, 9–10). There are several Greek words for a servant; this one (*doulos*) means a slave. An employee can quit, but a slave belongs to his master and must subordinate his will to his master's. Jesus chose this word in a Jewish context. Judaism grew up among empires ruled by authoritarian kings. Throughout the Middle East, everyone from the highest official to the lowest drudge was a slave with respect to the king. Thus, the Jews had no trouble imagining God as a monarch with absolute power over his subjects. In Greek translations of the Old Testament, *doulos* was used of God's greatest servants, such as Moses and the prophets (Joshua 14:7, 2 Kings 17:23).

"[T]he Israelite was conscious of the infinite distance between him and his God and also of his complete dependence upon him." Also, because the Lord was his people's Savior as well as Master, "the concept of the *doulos* still retained the element of unconditional subjection to another . . . yet lost the character of abject baseness. As a result of God's special election, *doulos* became a title of honour."[3]

Both Jesus and Paul observed that those who reject this monarch's rule do not thereby become free. On the contrary, "Everyone who sins is a slave to sin" (Jesus in John 8:34; compare Paul in Romans 6:16–18). In seeking to fulfill his own potential in his own way, this "independent" person ends up enslaved to a code of rules (Romans 7:6), a frantic effort to evade death (Hebrews

---

[3] R. Tuente, "Servant," *The New International Dictionary of New Testament Theology*, CD-ROM version (Grand Rapids: Zondervan, 1999).

2:15), or personal desires that become ever more compulsive (Romans 16:18; Titus 3:3). Anyone who has ever lost control of his eating, his temper, his spending, or some other habit knows how enslaving habits can be. On our own, the best we can do is break free of one compulsive approach to life, only to become enslaved to another.

But if God is just as exacting a master, is he really an improvement? Ultimately, each of us must answer that question for ourselves. To do so, the best place to look is at Jesus. The Son of God set aside the rights of divinity and took on the form of a slave for our sake (Philippians 2:7; compare Isaiah 53). The monarch stooped to serve the slave.

PRAYER AND PRAISE REPORT

Briefly share your prayer requests with the large group, making notations below. Then gather in smaller groups of two to four to pray for each other.

Date: _____

Prayer Requests

_____

_____

_____

_____

_____

_____

_____

_____

_____

Praise Report

_____

_____

_____

_____

_____

_____

_____

_____

_____

_____

REFLECTIONS

Use this page to write out your prayers, your thoughts about your daily Bible reading, or your meditations on a verse from the passage you have already studied. Below are some suggested verses for meditation. The Bible Reading Plan is on pages 87–88.

For Meditation: Luke 17:10 or Romans 6:16

For Gospel Reading:

- What do I *learn* from the life of Christ (his identity, personality, priorities)?

- How does he want me to *live* differently?

DVD NOTES

If you are watching the accompanying *Serving Like Christ Together* DVD, write down what you sense God saying to you through the speaker. (If you'd like to hear a sample of the DVD teaching segment, go to www.lifeto-gether.com/ExperiencingChristTogether.)

_____

_____

_____

_____

_____

_____

_____

_____

_____

_____

_____

_____

_____

_____

_____

_____

_____

_____

_____

_____

_____

_____

_____

_____

_____

_____

_____

_____

SESSION 6 · SERVING OUTSIDERS

Amanda agreed to host and lead a small group for six weeks. She wrote to her pastor: "I feel so inadequate and over my head. Here are these suffering people with so much pain and varying types of anger, and they have been meeting in my home. I have been praying for God's presence in my house and have been trying not to 'save' the people in my group.... The wonderful thing is that they are all in my little condo complex and didn't know each other before."

Even though she felt inadequate and scared, Amanda didn't let those feelings paralyze her. She kept opening her home to people she hadn't known before, even people she wouldn't have chosen as friends, because she was committed to serving Christ through true hospitality.

CONNECTING WITH GOD'S FAMILY   10 min.

1. This study has focused on the challenging things Jesus said and demonstrated about service. As you look back at the five previous sessions, what have been the high points or "aha!" moments for you?

   Or,

2. Meet with your spiritual partner(s). What have been the high points of your personal study, prayer, and or action during the past five weeks?

GROWING TO BE LIKE CHRIST   30 min.

Many of us find it's easier to serve some people than others. For example, some of us love to entertain, to have our friends over for a dinner or party. Throwing a party is a lot of work, but we get the benefit of social interaction and our friends' appreciation. On the other hand, who wants to serve their most annoying neighbors? The

lady at church who never seems to go away, the difficult person at work, the homeless, drug addicts, irritating relatives, persons from social classes or ethnic groups other than our own—most of us have an unwritten list of people we prefer not to serve. Jesus invites us to widen our circle of service to include those on our unwritten lists.

3. Read Luke 14:12–14. Why doesn't entertaining our friends, rich neighbors, or well-connected business contacts count as service (verse 12)?

4. Why do you suppose God will bless us for offering hospitality to "the poor, the crippled, the lame, the blind"?

5. How motivating is it for you personally when Jesus promises, "You will be repaid at the resurrection of the righteous"? Why do you feel that way? (You may want to consult the Study Notes.)

6. What's the connection between Luke 14:11 and 14:12–14?

7. Who are the people in your world who come to mind when you think of "the poor, the crippled, the lame, the blind"? (Again, consult the Study Notes.)

8. Read Luke 6:32–36. Here Jesus asks us to serve even people who don't like us. What reasons does he give?

9. Who are the people who come to mind when you think of those who don't love you, the ungrateful, and the wicked?

10. In what specific ways could you serve the people you identified in questions 7 and 9?

FOR DEEPER STUDY

Hospitality was extremely important in Jesus' day. Read Romans 12:13; Hebrews 13:1–3; and 1 Peter 4:9. Why do you suppose hospitality was so important? How is hospitality different from entertaining?

Read 1 Corinthians 3:10–15. What kinds of work or service do you think qualify as gold, silver, or costly stones? What does it mean to build on the foundation of Christ, as opposed to some other foundation? What do you think it will be like for those who are saved but whose entire work on earth is consumed by the flames because it has no lasting worth?

What else do you learn about our eternal destiny from 1 Corinthians 15:42–44, 51–54; 2 Corinthians 5:1–10; and 1 Thessalonians 4:16–17? How motivating is it for you here and now to think about your eternal destiny?

DEVELOPING YOUR GIFTS FOR SERVICE   20 min.

11. Our culture tends to be driven, focused on productivity and performance. We can easily think of service in that light: here are more tasks for you to do, more expectations that you must meet, more areas where you need to perform well in order to win God's approval. How can you serve people without being driven, overwhelmed, or compelled to perform up to an unreasonable standard?

12. If you haven't already done your service project, make your final plans now. If you've done your project, celebrate! In addition to having a good time, you can talk about what went well and what you learned.

SURRENDERING YOUR LIFE FOR GOD'S PLEASURE   15–30 min.

13. Will your group continue to meet after this session? If so, take a moment to write down the name of one friend that you want to bring to this group someday. Share that name with the group, have one person write down every name, and have another person pray for each name.

14. Turn to your Prayer and Praise Report on page 68. Which prayers has God answered? For what can you thank him?

STUDY NOTES

The poor, the crippled, the lame, the blind (Luke 14:13). In Jesus' day, respectable people often avoided the disabled because they viewed the disabled as inferior and impure. The law for priests in Leviticus 21:16–21, which said that priests had to be physically perfect as a symbol of God's perfection, was misinterpreted to include ordinary men and women. People thought disabilities indicated spiritual flaws. Jesus was urging his followers to extend hospitality to the needy, the disabled, and even those whose lives seemed to be a mess. Our desire for purity should not get in the way of our love.

Repaid at the resurrection (14:14). Jesus promises rewards to those who serve on his behalf. He doesn't spell out the details of what those rewards will be like. In 1 Corinthians 3:10–15, Paul suggests that anything we've done that is good and rooted in Christ will somehow last into eternity and bring us a reward. If we long to make our lives count, service is the way to go.

PRAYER AND PRAISE REPORT

Briefly share your prayer requests with the large group, making notations below. Then gather in smaller groups of two to four to pray for each other.

Date: _____

Prayer Requests

_____

_____

_____

_____

_____

_____

_____

_____

_____

Praise Report

_____

_____

_____

_____

_____

_____

_____

_____

_____

_____

REFLECTIONS

Use this page to write out your prayers, your thoughts about your daily Bible reading, or your meditations on a verse from the passage you have already studied. Below are some suggested verses for meditation. The Bible Reading Plan is on pages 87–88.

For Meditation: Luke 14:13–14

For Gospel Reading:

- What do I *learn* from the life of Christ (his identity, personality, priorities)?

- How does he want me to *live* differently?

DVD NOTES

If you are watching the accompanying *Serving Like Christ Together* DVD, write down what you sense God saying to you through the speaker. (If you'd like to hear a sample of the DVD teaching segment, go to www.lifeto-gether.com/ExperiencingChristTogether.)

FREQUENTLY ASKED QUESTIONS

What do we do on the first night of our group?

Like all fun things in life—have a party! A "get to know you" coffee, dinner, or dessert is a great way to launch a new study. You may want to review the LIFE TOGETHER Agreement (pages 74–75) and share the names of a few friends you can invite to join you. But most importantly, have fun before your study time begins.

Where do we find new members for our group?

This can be troubling, especially for new groups that have only a few people or for existing groups that lose a few people along the way. We encourage you to pray with your group and then brainstorm a list of people from work, church, your neighborhood, your children's school, family, the gym, and so forth. Then have each group member invite several of the people on his or her list. Another good strategy is to ask church leaders to make an announcement or allow a bulletin insert.

No matter how you find members, it's vital that you stay on the lookout for new people to join your group. All groups tend to go through healthy attrition—the result of moves, releasing new leaders, ministry opportunities, and so forth—and if the group gets too small, it could be at risk of shutting down. If you and your group stay open, you'll be amazed at the people God sends your way. The next person just might become a friend for life. You never know!

How long will this group meet?

It's totally up to the group—once you come to the end of this six-week study. Most groups meet weekly for at least the first six weeks, but every other week can work as well. We strongly recommend that the group meet for the first six months on a weekly basis if at all possible. This allows for continuity, and if people miss a meeting they aren't gone for a whole month.

At the end of this study, each group member may decide if he or she wants to continue on for another six-week study. Some groups launch relationships for years to come, and others are stepping-stones into another group experience. Either way, enjoy the journey.

Can we do this study on our own?

Absolutely! This may sound crazy but one of the best ways to do this study is not with a full house but with a few friends. You may choose to gather with one other couple who would enjoy going to the movies or having a quiet dinner and then walking through this study. Jesus will be with you even if there are only two of you (Matthew 18:20).

What if this group is not working for us?

You're not alone! This could be the result of a personality conflict, life stage difference, geographical distance, level of spiritual maturity, or any number of things. Relax. Pray for God's direction, and at the end of this six-week study, decide whether to continue with this group or find another. You don't buy the first car you look at or marry the first person you date, and the same goes with a group. Don't bail out before the six weeks are up—God might have something to teach you. Also, don't run from conflict or prejudge people before you have given them a chance. God is still working in you too!

Who is the leader?

Most groups have an official leader. But ideally, the group will mature and members will rotate the leadership of meetings. We have discovered that healthy groups rotate hosts/leaders and homes on a regular basis. This model ensures that all members grow, give their unique contribution, and develop their gifts. This study guide and the Holy Spirit can keep things on track even when you rotate leaders. Christ has promised to be in your midst as you gather. Ultimately, God is your leader each step of the way.

How do we handle the child care needs in our group?

Very carefully. Seriously, this can be a sensitive issue. We suggest that you empower the group to openly brainstorm solutions. You may try one option that works for a while and then adjust over time. Our favorite approach is for adults to meet in the living room or dining room, and to share the cost of a babysitter (or two) who can be with the kids in a different part of the house. In this way, parents don't have to be away from their children all evening when their children are too young to be left at home. A second option is to use one home for the kids and a second home (close by or a phone call away) for the adults. A third idea is to rotate the responsibility of providing a lesson or care for the children either in the same home or in another home nearby. This can be an incredible blessing for kids. Finally, the most common idea is to decide that you need to have a night to invest in your spiritual lives individually or as a couple, and to make your own arrangements for child care. No matter what decision the group makes, the best approach is to dialogue openly about both the problem and the solution.

To answer your further questions, we have created a website called www.lifetogether.com/ExperiencingChristTogether that can be your small group coach. Here are ten reasons to check out this website:

1. Top twenty questions every new leader asks
2. Common problems most new leaders face and ways to overcome them
3. Seven steps to building a healthy small group in six weeks
4. Free downloadable resources and leadership support
5. Additional leadership training material for every lesson in the EXPERIENCING CHRIST TOGETHER series
6. Ten stories from leaders who successfully completed this study
7. Free chat rooms and bulletin boards
8. Downloadable Health Assessments and Health Plans for individuals or groups
9. A chance to join a community of small group leaders by affinity, geography, or denominational affiliation
10. Best of all, a free newsletter with the best ideas from leaders around the world

LIFE TOGETHER AGREEMENT

OUR PURPOSE

To transform our spiritual lives by cultivating our spiritual health in a healthy small group community. In addition, we: _____

_____

_____.

OUR VALUES

Group Attendance	To give priority to the group meeting. We will call or email if we will be late or absent. (Completing the Small Group Calendar on page 76 will minimize this issue.)
Safe Environment	To help create a safe place where people can be heard and feel loved. (Please, no quick answers, snap judgments, or simple fixes.)
Respect Differences	To be gentle and gracious to people with different spiritual maturity, personal opinions, temperaments, or imperfections. We are all works in progress.
Confidentiality	To keep anything that is shared strictly confidential and within the group, and to avoid sharing improper information about those outside the group.
Encouragement for Growth	To be not just takers but givers of life. We want to spiritually multiply our life by serving others with our God-given gifts.
Welcome for Newcomers	To keep an open chair and share Jesus' dream of finding a shepherd for every sheep.
Shared Ownership	To remember that every member is a minister and to ensure that each attender will share a

	small team role or responsibility over time. (See Team Roles on pages 77–79.)
Rotating Hosts/Leaders and Homes	To encourage different people to host the group in their homes, and to rotate the responsibility of facilitating each meeting. (See the Small Group Calendar on page 76.)

OUR EXPECTATIONS

• Refreshments/mealtimes _____

• Child care _____

• When we will meet (day of week) _____

• Where we will meet (place) _____

• We will begin at (time)_____ and end at _____

• We will do our best to have some or all of us attend a worship service
  together. Our primary worship service time will be _____

• Date of this agreement _____

• Date we will review this agreement again _____

• Who (other than the leader) will review this agreement at the end of this
  study_____

SMALL GROUP CALENDAR

Planning and calendaring can help ensure the greatest participation at every meeting. At the end of each meeting, review this calendar. Be sure to include a regular rotation of host homes and leaders, and don't forget birthdays, socials, church events, holidays, and mission/ministry projects. Go to www.lifetogether.com for an electronic copy of this form and more than a hundred ideas for your group to do together.

Date	Lesson	Host Home	Dessert/Meal	Leader
Monday, January 15	1	Steve and Laura's	Joe	Bill

TEAM ROLES

APPENDIX

The Bible makes clear that every member, not just the small group leader, is a minister in the body of Christ. In a healthy small group, every member takes on some small role or responsibility. It's more fun and effective if you team up on these roles.

Review the team roles and responsibilities below, and have each member volunteer for a role or participate on a team. If someone doesn't know where to serve or is holding back, have the group suggest a team or role. It's best to have one or two people on each team so you have each of the five purposes covered. Serving in even a small capacity will not only help your leader but also will make the group more fun for everyone. Don't hold back. Join a team!

The opportunities below are broken down by the five purposes and then by a *crawl* (beginning step), *walk* (intermediate step), or *run* (advanced step). Try to cover at least the crawl and walk roles, and select a role that matches your group, your gifts, and your maturity. If you can't find a good step or just want to see other ideas, go to www.lifetogether.com and see what other groups are choosing.

Team Roles	Team Player(s)

CONNECTING TEAM (Fellowship and Community Building)

Crawl:	Host a social event or group activity in the first week or two.	_____ _____
Walk:	Create a list of uncommitted members and then invite them to an open house or group social.	_____ _____
Run:	Plan a twenty-four-hour retreat or weekend getaway for the group. Lead the Connecting time each week for the group.	_____ _____

GROWING TEAM (Discipleship and Spiritual Growth)

Crawl: Coordinate the spiritual partners for the
group. Facilitate a three- or four-person
discussion circle during the Bible study
portion of your meeting. Coordinate the
discussion circles.

_____

_____

Walk: Tabulate the Personal Health Assessments
and Health Plans in a summary to let
people know how you're doing as a group.
Encourage personal devotions through group discussions
and pairing up with spiritual (accountability) partners.

_____

_____

Run: Take the group on a prayer walk, or plan
a day of solitude, fasting, or personal retreat.

_____

_____

SERVING TEAM (Discovering Your God-Given Design for Ministry)

Crawl: Ensure that every member finds a
group role or team he or she enjoys.

_____

_____

Walk: Have every member take a gift test
(see www.lifetogether.com) and
determine your group's gifts. Plan a
ministry project together.

_____

_____

Run: Help each member decide on a
way to use his or her unique gifts
somewhere in the church.

_____

_____

SHARING TEAM (Sharing and Evangelism)

Crawl: Coordinate the group's Prayer and
Praise Report of friends and family
who don't know Christ.

_____

_____

Walk: Search for group mission opportunities
and plan a cross-cultural group activity.

_____

_____

Run: Take a small-group "vacation" to host a
six-week group in your neighborhood
or office. Then come back together
with your current group.

_____

_____

SURRENDERING TEAM (Surrendering Your Heart to Worship)

Crawl: Maintain the group's Prayer
and Praise Report or journal.

          _____

Walk: Lead a brief time of worship each
week (at the beginning or end of
your meeting), either a cappella or
using a song from the DVD or the
LIFE TOGETHER Worship DVD/CD.

Run: Plan a unique time of worship through
Communion, foot washing, night of
prayer, or nature walking.

PERSONAL HEALTH ASSESSMENT

	Just Beginning	Getting Going	Well Developed

CONNECTING WITH GOD AND OTHERS

I am deepening my understanding of and friendship
with God in community with others. — 1 2 3 4 5

I am growing in my ability both to share and to
show my love to others. — 1 2 3 4 5

I am willing to share my real needs for prayer and
support from others. — 1 2 3 4 5

I am resolving conflict constructively and am
willing to forgive others. — 1 2 3 4 5

CONNECTING Total _____

GROWING IN YOUR SPIRITUAL JOURNEY

I have a growing relationship with God through regular
time in the Bible and in prayer (spiritual habits). — 1 2 3 4 5

I am experiencing more of the characteristics of
Jesus Christ (love, patience, gentleness, courage,
self-control, and so forth) in my life. — 1 2 3 4 5

I am avoiding addictive behaviors (food, television,
busyness, and the like) to meet my needs. — 1 2 3 4 5

I am spending time with a Christian friend (spiritual partner)
who celebrates and challenges my spiritual growth. — 1 2 3 4 5

GROWING Total _____

SERVING WITH YOUR GOD-GIVEN DESIGN

I have discovered and am further developing my
unique God-given design. — 1 2 3 4 5

I am regularly praying for God to show me
opportunities to serve him and others. — 1 2 3 4 5

I am serving in a regular (once a month or more)
ministry in the church or community. — 1 2 3 4 5

I am a team player in my small group by sharing
some group role or responsibility. — 1 2 3 4 5

SERVING Total _____

SHARING GOD'S LOVE IN EVERYDAY LIFE

	Just Beginning	Getting Going	Well Developed
I am cultivating relationships with non-Christians and praying for God to give me natural opportunities to share his love.		1 2 3 4 5	
I am praying and learning about where God can use me and my group cross-culturally for missions.		1 2 3 4 5	
I am investing my time in another person or group who needs to know Christ.		1 2 3 4 5	
I am regularly inviting unchurched or unconnected friends to my church or small group.		1 2 3 4 5	

SHARING Total _____

SURRENDERING YOUR LIFE TO GOD

I am experiencing more of the presence and power of God in my everyday life.	1 2 3 4 5
I am faithfully attending services and my small group to worship God.	1 2 3 4 5
I am seeking to please God by surrendering every area of my life (health, decisions, finances, relationships, future, and the like) to him.	1 2 3 4 5
I am accepting the things I cannot change and becoming increasingly grateful for the life I've been given.	1 2 3 4 5

SURRENDERING Total _____

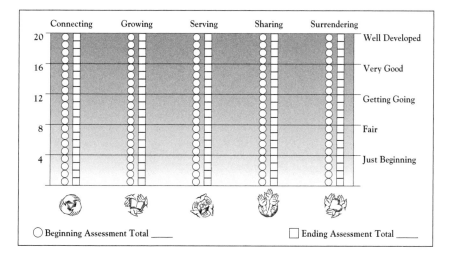

Beginning Assessment Total _____   Ending Assessment Total _____

PERSONAL
HEALTH PLAN

This worksheet could become your single most important feature in this study. On it you can record your personal priorities before the Father. It will help you live a healthy spiritual life, balancing all five of God's purposes.

PURPOSE	PLAN
CONNECT	WHO are you connecting with spiritually?
GROW	WHAT is your next step for growth?
DEVELOP	WHERE are you serving?
SHARE	WHEN are you shepherding another in Christ?
SURRENDER	HOW are you surrendering your heart?

Additional copies of the Personal Health Plan may be downloaded in a larger format at www.lifetogether.com/healthplan.

DATE	MY PROGRESS	PARTNER'S PROGRESS

SAMPLE PERSONAL HEALTH PLAN

This worksheet could become your single most important feature in this study. On it you can record your personal priorities before the Father. It will help you live a healthy spiritual life, balancing all five of God's purposes.

PURPOSE	PLAN
CONNECT	WHO are you connecting with spiritually? *Bill and I will meet weekly by email or phone.*
GROW	WHAT is your next step for growth? *Regular devotions or journaling my prayers 2x/week*
DEVELOP	WHERE are you serving? *Serving in Children's Ministry* *Go through GIFTS class*
SHARE	WHEN are you shepherding another in Christ? *Shepherding Bill at lunch or hosting a starter group in the fall*
SURRENDER	HOW are you surrendering your heart? *Help with our teenager* *New job situation*

DATE	MY PROGRESS	PARTNER'S PROGRESS
3/5	Talked during our group	Figured out our goals together
3/12	Missed our time together	Missed our time together
3/26	Met for coffee and review of my goals	Met for coffee
4/10	Emailed prayer requests	Bill sent me his prayer requests
3/5	Great start on personal journaling	Read Mark 1–6 in one sitting!
3/12	Traveled and not doing well this week	Journaled about Christ as Healer
3/26	Back on track	Busy and distracted; asked for prayer
3/1	Need to call Children's Pastor	
3/26	Group did a serving project together	Agreed to lead group worship
3/30	Regularly rotating leadership	Led group worship—great job!
3/5	Called Jim to see if he's open to joining our group	Wanted to invite somebody, but didn't
3/12	Preparing to start a group this fall	
3/30	Group prayed for me	Told friend something he's learning about Christ
3/5	Overwhelmed but encouraged	Scared to lead worship
3/15	Felt heard and more settled	Issue with wife
3/30	Read book on teens	Glad he took on his fear

JOURNALING 101

Henri Nouwen says effective and lasting ministry *for* God grows out of a quiet place alone *with* God. This is why journaling is so important.

The greatest adventure of our lives is found in the daily pursuit of knowing, growing in, serving, sharing, and worshiping Christ forever. This is the essence of a purposeful life: to see all five biblical purposes fully formed and balanced in our lives. Only then are we "complete in Christ" (Colossians 1:28, NASB).

David poured his heart out to God by writing psalms. The book of Psalms contains many of his honest conversations with God in written form, including expressions of every imaginable emotion on every aspect of his life. Like David, we encourage you to select a strategy to integrate God's Word and journaling into your devotional time. Use any of the following resources:

- Bible
- One-year Bible
- New Testament Bible Challenge Reading Plan (www.lifetogether.com/readingprograms)
- Devotional book
- Topical Bible study plan

Before or after you read a portion of God's Word, speak to God in honest reflection or response in the form of a written prayer. You may begin this time by simply finishing the sentence "Father . . . ," "Yesterday Lord . . . ,"or "Thank you, God, for. . . ." Share with him where you are at the present moment; express your hurts, disappointments, frustrations, blessings, victories, gratefulness. Whatever you do with your journal, make a plan that fits you so you'll have a positive experience. Consider sharing highlights of your progress and experiences with some or all of your group members, especially your spiritual partner(s). You may find they want to join and even encourage you in this journey. Most of all, enjoy the ride and cultivate a more authentic, growing walk with God.

BIBLE READING PLAN

30 Days through the Gospel of Matthew

Imagine sitting at the feet of Jesus himself: the Teacher who knows how to live life well, the Savior who died for you, the Lord who commands the universe. Like his first disciples, you can follow him around, watch what he does, listen to what he says, and pattern your life after his.

On the next page is a plan for reading through the gospel of Matthew. Matthew's is the most Jewish of the four gospels. He wants us to understand that Jesus didn't come out of nowhere—for centuries God had been laying the groundwork for Jesus' mission. That groundwork was the Jewish people and the Jewish Scriptures (the Old Testament). Some of that Jewish background, like the genealogy that dominates Matthew 1, may not interest you. But as you read, keep asking yourself: *How did Jesus fulfill God's age-old promises of a King who would reign with justice? How does Jesus the King want me— a citizen of his kingdom—to live?*

Find a quiet place, and have ready a notebook or journal in which you can write what you learn and what you want to say back to God. You may also use the Reflection pages at the end of each session of this study. It's helpful to have one or two simple questions in mind to focus your reading. In addition to the two above, here are some suggestions:

- What do I learn from the life of Christ (his identity, personality, priorities)?

- How does he want me to live differently?

When we've sat at the Master's feet like this ourselves, the sense of a real, alive, present Jesus has been breathtaking. We pray you'll have the same experience.

- ☐ Day 1   Matthew 1–2
- ☐ Day 2   Matthew 3
- ☐ Day 3   Matthew 4
- ☐ Day 4   Matthew 5:1–20
- ☐ Day 5   Matthew 5:21–48
- ☐ Day 6   Matthew 6
- ☐ Day 7   Matthew 7
- ☐ Day 8   Matthew 8
- ☐ Day 9   Matthew 9
- ☐ Day 10 Matthew 10
- ☐ Day 11 Matthew 11
- ☐ Day 12 Matthew 12:1–21
- ☐ Day 13 Matthew 12:22–50
- ☐ Day 14 Matthew 13:1–30
- ☐ Day 15 Matthew 13:31–58
- ☐ Day 16 Matthew 14
- ☐ Day 17 Matthew 15
- ☐ Day 18 Matthew 16
- ☐ Day 19 Matthew 17
- ☐ Day 20 Matthew 18
- ☐ Day 21 Matthew 19
- ☐ Day 22 Matthew 20
- ☐ Day 23 Matthew 21
- ☐ Day 24 Matthew 22
- ☐ Day 25 Matthew 23
- ☐ Day 26 Matthew 24
- ☐ Day 27 Matthew 25
- ☐ Day 28 Matthew 26
- ☐ Day 29 Matthew 27
- ☐ Day 30 Matthew 28

LEADING FOR THE FIRST TIME

- **Sweaty palms are a healthy sign.** The Bible says God is gracious to the humble. Remember who is in control; the time to worry is when you're not worried. Those who are soft in heart (and sweaty-palmed) are those whom God is sure to speak through.

- **Seek support.** Ask your leader, coleader, or close friend to pray for you and prepare with you before the session. Walking through the study will help you anticipate potentially difficult questions and discussion topics.

- **Bring your uniqueness to the study.** Lean into who you are and how God wants you to uniquely lead the study.

- **Prepare. Prepare. Prepare.** Go through the session several times. If you are using the DVD, listen to the teaching segment and Leadership Lifter. Go to www.lifetogether.com and download pertinent files. Consider writing in a journal or fasting for a day to prepare yourself for what God wants to do.

- **Don't wait until the last minute to prepare.**

- **Ask for feedback so you can grow.** Perhaps in an email or on cards handed out at the study, have everyone write down three things you did well and one thing you could improve on. Don't get defensive, but show an openness to learn and grow.

- **Use online resources.** Go to www.lifetogether.com and listen to Brett Eastman share the weekly Leadership Lifter and download any additional notes or ideas for your session. You may also want to subscribe to the DOING LIFE TOGETHER Newsletter and LLT Newsletter. Both can be obtained for free by signing up at www.lifetogether.com/subscribe.

- **Prayerfully consider launching a new group.** This doesn't need to happen overnight, but God's heart is for this to happen over time. Not all

Christians are called to be leaders or teachers, but we are all called to be "shepherds" of a few someday.

- **Share with your group what God is doing in your heart.** God is searching for those whose hearts are fully his. Share your trials and victories. We promise that people will relate.

- **Prayerfully consider whom you would like to pass the baton to next week.** It's only fair. God is ready for the next member of your group to go on the faith journey you just traveled. Make it fun, and expect God to do the rest.

HOSTING AN OPEN HOUSE

If you're starting a new group, try planning an "open house" before your first formal group meeting. Even if you only have two to four core members, it's a great way to break the ice and to consider prayerfully who else might be open to join you over the next few weeks. You can also use this kick-off meeting to hand out study guides, spend some time getting to know each other, discuss each person's expectations for the group, and briefly pray for each other.

A simple meal or good desserts always make a kick-off meeting more fun. After people introduce themselves and share how they ended up being at the meeting (you can play a game to see who has the wildest story!), have everyone respond to a few icebreaker questions: "What is your favorite family vacation?" or "What is one thing you love about your church/our community?" or "What are three things about your life growing up that most people here don't know?" See www.lifetogether.com for more icebreaker ideas.

Next, ask everyone to tell what he or she hopes to get out of the study. You might want to review the LIFE TOGETHER Agreement (pages 74–75) and talk about each person's expectations and priorities.

Finally, set an open chair (maybe two) in the center of your group and explain that it represents someone who would enjoy or benefit from this group but who isn't here yet. Ask people to pray about whom they could invite to join the group over the next few weeks. Hand out postcards (see www.lifeto-gether.com for examples) and have everyone write an invitation or two. Don't worry about ending up with too many people—you can always have one discussion circle in the living room and another in the dining room after you watch the lesson. Each group could then report prayer requests and progress at the end of the session.

You can skip this kick-off meeting if your time is limited, but you'll experience a huge benefit if you take the time to connect with each other in this way.

EXPERIENCING CHRIST TOGETHER IN A SUNDAY SCHOOL SETTING

Sunday school is one of the best places to begin building community in your church, and the EXPERIENCING CHRIST TOGETHER DVDs and study guides work in concert to help your Sunday school leadership team do it easily and effectively.

Each study guide of the LIFE TOGETHER curriculum includes a companion DVD with today's top Christian leaders speaking to the passage of Scripture under discussion. Here is one way to use the DVD in a Sunday school class:

- Moderator introduction: welcome the class, and read the Scripture passage for the session
- DVD teaching segment: ten to fifteen minutes
- Small group discussion: divide into small groups of eight to twelve and, using the questions from the curriculum, discuss how the passage applies to each person in the class

So often Sunday school consists of the star teacher with little involvement from others. To use the EXPERIENCING CHRIST TOGETHER DVDs effectively means recruiting a host of people to participate in the Sunday school program. We recommend four teams:

Moderators. These are the facilitators or leaders of the class. Their role is to transition the class through each step in the time together. For example, the moderator will welcome the class and open with prayer. In addition, he or she will introduce the DVD segment by reading the Scripture passage for the session. We recommend that you recruit several moderaters. That allows you to rotate the moderators each week. Doing so takes the pressure off people to commit to every week of the class—and it offers more people opportunity for upfront leadership. One church recruited three sets of moderators (a total of six) because the Sunday school leaders wanted to use the curriculum for twelve weeks. They knew that out of twelve weeks, one set of moderators would, likely, burn out; it's difficult for anyone to provide leadership for twelve straight weeks.

Discussion Guides. These are people who lead the follow-up discussion after the DVD teaching segment. If, for example, your Sunday school runs for an hour, you may want to plan on fifteen to twenty minutes for the DVD teaching segment and an additional twenty to thirty minutes in small group discussion afterward. One church recruited many of its seniors to lead the discussion groups. Some of them had felt excluded from ministry, and the role of discussion guide opened the door for them to serve.

Each discussion guide needs only to read through the passage and the questions in each study guide for preparation. After the DVD teaching segment, the moderator of the class asks the discussion guides to stand up. Then, people circle their chairs around each discussion guide. It's an easy way to create small groups each week. You may need to help some groups find more people or other groups to divide once more, if they end up too large. One church asked some of the discussion guides to move their groups into different rooms, because the seniors had a hard time hearing.

Hospitality Coordinators. These are those who oversee the food and drink for the class. Some classes may not provide this, but for those who do, it's important that multiple people join the team, so one or two people don't burn out over the course of the class.

Technical Coordinators. There's nothing worse than a DVD player that doesn't seem to work. Recruit at least one person to oversee making sure the DVD works each week. It's best, though, to recruit two or three people, in order to rotate them throughout the Sunday school series. It's important that the technical team has made sure the DVD player works *before* the class begins.

One church decided to gather all the adult Sunday school classes together for a twelve-week series using the Life Together DVD and study guides. What happened was amazing—instead of Sunday school starting off with 140 people and ending up with half that many at the end of the fall, attendance stayed high the entire time. Instead of one Sunday school class being led by one or two teachers, more than thirty-five people were involved in some kind of leadership—as moderators, discussion guides, hospitality (food) coordinators, or technical coordinators. The fifteen-minute time at the beginning of Sunday school for coffee and snacks (fruit, coffee cake, etc.) proved just as valuable as the content portion!

The fall program gave the church a new vision for how Sunday school can support the larger issue of spiritual formation and life change. For more ideas and practical tools to strengthen your small group ministry, go to www.lifetogethertoday.com.

INTRODUCTION

If your group is new, or even if you haven't been together for a few weeks, we recommend that you plan a kick-off meeting where you will pray, hand out study guides, spend some time getting to know each other, and discuss each person's expectations for the group. A meeting like this is a great way to start a group or step up people's commitments.

Most groups, if reconvened after a short break, will be renewed in seeing each other and open to increasing their commitment as much as 25 percent. We have seen some naturally move to a weekly format, begin doing homework, and commit to daily devotions simply because the leader shared his or her heart. What do you sense God wants from you and your group?

However, if your group is brand new, a simple meal, potluck, or even good desserts make a kick-off meeting more fun. After dessert, have everyone respond to an icebreaker question, such as, "How did you hear of this church, and what's one thing you love about it?" Or, "Tell us three things about your life growing up that most people here don't know."

Then ask everyone to tell what he or she hopes to get out of this study. You might want to review the LIFE TOGETHER Agreement (see pages 74–75) and talk about each person's expectations and priorities. You could discuss whether you want to do Bible study homework before each meeting—homework covering the questions under Growing and/or the For Deeper Study sections. Review the Small Group Calendar on page 76 and talk about who else is willing to open their home or facilitate a meeting.

Finally, cast the vision, as Jesus did, to be inclusive not exclusive. Ask everyone to prayerfully think of people who would enjoy or benefit from a group like this. The beginning of a new study is a great time to welcome a few people into your circle. Have each person share a name or two and either make phone calls the coming week or handwrite invitations or postcards that very night. This will make it fun and also make it happen. At www.lifeto gether.com we have a free email invitation you may send to every potential member. Don't worry about ending up with too many people—you can always have one discussion circle in the living room and another in the dining room.

SESSION ONE:
WHAT IS SUCCESS?

As a leader, your most important job is to create an atmosphere where people are willing to talk honestly about what Christ's words and actions have to do with them. Especially if your group is new, be available before people arrive so you can greet them at the door. People are naturally nervous at a new group, so a hug or handshake can help put them at ease.

You may ask a few people to come early to help set up, pray, and introduce newcomers to others. Even if everyone is new, they don't know that yet and may be shy when they arrive. You might give people roles like setting up nametags or handing out drinks. This could be a great way to spot a coleader.

Because this study is about servanthood, it's a great chance for you to lead by example. Look for ways to be a servant leader.

Question 1. You should be the first to answer this question while others are thinking about how to respond. Be sure to give everyone a chance to respond to this question, because it's a chance for the group to get to know each other. It's not necessary to go around the circle in order. Just ask for volunteers.

Introduction to the Series. If this is your first LIFE TOGETHER study, take a moment after question 1 to orient the group to one principle that undergirds this series: *A healthy small group balances the purposes of the church.* Most small groups emphasize Bible study, fellowship, and prayer. But God has called us to reach out to others as well. He wants us to *do* what Jesus teaches, not just *learn about* it. You may spend less time in this series studying the Bible than some group members are used to. That's because you'll spend more time doing things the Bible says believers should do.

However, those who like more Bible study can find plenty of it in this series. At the end of each session, For Deeper Study provides more passages you can study on the same topic. If your group likes to do deeper Bible study, consider having members answer next week's Growing section questions ahead of time as homework. They can even study next week's For Deeper Study passages for homework too. Then, during the Growing portion of your meeting, you can share the high points of what you've learned.

If the five biblical purposes are new to your group, be sure to review them together on pages 8–10 of the Read Me First section.

Question 2. An agreement helps you clarify your group's priorities and cast new vision for what the group can be. Members can imagine what your group could be like if they lived these values. So turn to pages 74–75 and choose one value that you want to emphasize in this study. We've suggested some options.

Question 3. Have someone read aloud the introductory paragraph and someone else read the Bible passage. It's a good idea to ask people ahead of time, because not everyone is comfortable reading aloud in public. When the passage has been read, ask question 3. *It is not necessary that everyone answer every question in the Bible study.* In fact, a group can become boring if you simply go around the circle and give answers. Your goal is to create a discussion— which means that perhaps only a few people respond to each question and an engaging dialogue gets going. It's even fine to skip some questions in order to spend more time on questions you believe are most important.

Also, we highly recommend that as leader, you read the Study Notes ahead of time each week and draw the group's attention to anything there that will help them understand the Bible passage.

Questions 3, 4, and 5. James and John thought status or the power to give orders was the sign of success or greatness. Lording over others, exercising authority (telling people what to do), and getting one's way were the signs of success then as now. As a follow-up question, you might ask what your group thinks it means to "lord over" someone.

Questions 6 and 7. Jesus' idea of greatness through servanthood ran against everything Roman culture believed. It was common for powerful people to "serve" their communities by supporting arts, sports, and religious events, but they got status and perks in exchange. The same is true today. Jesus is talking about ceasing to see oneself as better than others, looking for ways to build others up and seek their good, and ceasing to look for ways to improve one's image. If we are leaders at work, at home, or in the church, we treat others with full respect and routinely treat their needs and desires as more important than our own.

Question 8. The costs of Jesus' approach can be high. We may not get promoted in our organization as high as we would have been if we focused on building up our image and undercutting others. We may make less money or get less applause. None of these costs is certain—servant leaders often win their colleagues' trust and are rewarded accordingly. But the risks are real. However, the benefits of a servant mindset are strong personal character, the respect of those who are wise, the enormous good we can do for others, and God's rejoicing.

Questions 9 and 10. It will be helpful if you think of answers ahead of time and share honestly with the group. Look around your life for a couple of days and notice the people who serve you in restaurants, behind the scenes at work, in stores, and so on. Who serves you? How do you treat them?

Question 12. We've offered several options for personal time with God, as well as some action items. Every believer should have a plan for personal time with God. Walk the group through these options. If group members have never read through the gospel of Matthew, we strongly urge that they select that option. This will immerse them in the person of Christ for the duration of this study. There's a blank page entitled Reflections at the end of every session for them to write down what they discover.

For those who have done a lot of Bible study, we encourage the meditation option. Living with one short passage each week can help them move biblical truth from their heads into their hearts and actions. The prayer option—whether five minutes a day or thirty—is valuable for anyone. We strongly suggest that those who have never used a personal prayer journal should give it a try.

Tell the group which option(s) you have chosen. Your willingness will be a model for them.

Question 13. For those who haven't done a LIFE TOGETHER study before, spiritual partners will be a new idea. We highly encourage you to try pairs or triplets for six weeks. It's so hard to start a spiritual practice like prayer or consistent Bible reading with no support. A friend makes a huge difference. Partners can check in with each other weekly, either at the beginning of your group meetings or outside the meeting.

SESSION TWO: SERVING CHRIST IN OTHERS

Questions 1 and 2. Checking in with your spiritual partners (question 2) will be an option in all sessions from now on. You'll need to watch the clock and keep these conversations to ten minutes. If partners want more time together (as is ideal), they can connect before, after, or outside meetings. Give them a two-minute notice and hold to it if you ever want to get them back in the circle! If some group members are absent or newcomers have joined you, you may need to help partnerless people connect with new or temporary partners.

If you prefer (and especially if there are many newcomers), question 1 will always be a lighter icebreaker for the whole group. We encourage you, though, to let partners check in at least every other week so that those relationships grow solid. Please don't miss this opportunity to take your people deeper. Remember that the goal here is "transforming lives through community," and one-on-one time has an enormous return on time spent. In a week or two, you might want to ask the group how their partnerships are going and what kind of progress is being made. This will encourage those who are struggling to connect or accomplish their goals.

Question 4. Christ says we need to see him in each believer (or possibly in every human being) and treat each person as we would treat him. Think of each person in your group in turn. How would you treat that person if he or she were Christ?

Question 6. You could have a lively discussion about hell. Jesus' description of eternal punishment is severe. Many people today think a loving God would not create that kind of hell and banish people to it. Pastors rarely preach on hell these days because it offends people. What do your group members believe about hell? You may need to cut this discussion short because it's not the main point of the passage. The main point is that Jesus will judge our lives by the ways we treat the neediest members of our communities.

Question 7. This question is more central to a discussion about servanthood. Talk about ways you could—as individuals and as a group—care for the neediest in your community.

Question 9. The time problem is really an issue of priorities. Most of us place highest priority on caring for our own needs and those of our loved ones.

That takes a lot of time, and little is left over. But you can choose as a group to plan time into each month to do something for those who aren't family or friends. In some cases you may choose to give money instead of time. However, the more you make service opportunities group activities instead of just occasions to pull out your checkbook, the more you will find them to be among the most spiritually stretching times of your small group experience. Besides, these times will help bond your group and likely be the source of great memories.

Questions 12 and 13. We strongly encourage an outward focus for your group because groups that become too inwardly focused tend to become unhealthy over time. People naturally gravitate to feeding themselves through Bible study, prayer, and social time, so it's usually up to the leader to push them to consider how this inward nourishment can overflow into outward service to others. Don't let this meeting end without a commitment from people to participate in a service project sometime in the next month.

Try to come to this question prepared to get the discussion started with your own ideas. Also, ask your pastor if there are any needs in the congregation that your group could fill: an elderly person who could use a Saturday morning yard cleanup, or someone just out of the hospital who isn't yet able to clean her house. Be sure to check out the website at www.lifetogether.com for twenty-five group serving ideas.

If no one volunteers to plan the service project, don't be discouraged. Who do you think are the one or two planners in your group? They are likely to respond well if you ask them right after your meeting to take on this project and if you ask two people to team up. Another surefire approach is to ask the group who would be two people perfect for this task. If the planners in your group have already planned another project recently, tap a couple of people who haven't had a chance to serve the group in this way.

SESSION THREE:
COMPASSION

In order to maximize your time together and honor the diversity of personality types, do your best to begin and end your group on time. You may even want to adjust your starting or stopping time. Don't hesitate to open in prayer even before everyone is seated. This isn't disrespectful of those who are still gathering—it respects those who are ready to begin, and the others won't be offended.

If you've had trouble getting through all of the Bible study questions, consider breaking into smaller circles of four or five people for the Bible study (Growing) portion of your meeting. Everyone will get more "airtime," and the people who tend to dominate the discussion will be balanced out. A circle of four doesn't need an experienced leader, and it's a great way to identify and train a coleader.

Question 4. They were "like sheep without a shepherd"—that is, they were lost, wandering, and vulnerable because they had no one to guide them, point them in the right direction, show them what really matters in life, help them clean up the mess in their lives, or give them hope and encouragement. In session 2 you saw the importance of caring for people's physical needs—food, clothing, and so on. But Jesus also had compassion for people's relational and spiritual needs. Prisoners needed someone to visit them (Matthew 25); everyone needed a shepherd.

Question 6. Jesus both fed people (physical needs) and taught them (spiritual needs). He served them as whole persons with bodies and spirits.

Question 7. Like the disciples, we often have less compassion when we believe there's nothing we can do for someone or when we're physically or emotionally exhausted. Rest is essential for creative thinking and compassionate response.

Question 8. If you experience compassion fatigue, be open about that with your group. Your openness will help others admit their own limitations.

Question 11. In a study about service, it's important to hold up the value of rest alongside the value of service. Each sustains the other. We need God's guidance to maintain a healthy balance.

Question 13. As leader, you're in the people development business. Part of your job is to help others discover and develop their gifts. You may not need their help to plan a service project or lead a meeting, but they need you to let them take on a role and support them so that they succeed. If you have children, you know that it's often easier to do a job yourself than to help someone else learn to do it. But that's what Jesus did with his disciples, and it's what he wants us to do for those we lead. If anyone in your group doesn't have even a small role in serving the group, engage group members in identifying an area of service that suits that person's abilities.

One important area of service is hosting the group. We strongly recommend you challenge your members to take whatever step that they sense God is calling them to and that will challenge them. You will need to motivate people because many people's default position is to let others do the work.

For some people, just exerting themselves enough to share in providing refreshments for the group or cleaning up after meetings would be a step forward. Others serve as a matter of course. You may want to call attention to those group members who have been serving your group in various ways during the past few meetings and thank them.

If you as leader have been doing all the serving in your group, this is the time to give others a chance. Ask for a volunteer to handle the group's Prayer and Praise Report and check in with those who have asked for prayer. Let people know they could plan worship for the group.

Finally, remind everyone to write down the prayers of each member as they are shared in the group. You could be missing out on the blessing of seeing prayers answered and the value of remembering each others' prayers.

SESSION FOUR:
THE HOLY SPIRIT

Question 3. Jesus says his disciples live in a world where true peace is rare and where hearts easily become troubled and fearful. For several years they have had Jesus himself to guide them, but now they'll need the Holy Spirit to remind them of what's real and what's important. The Spirit wants to help us know who, when, and how to serve.

Question 5. Surprisingly, loving and serving one another increases our experience of the Holy Spirit. The Spirit is our guide in how to serve people, and he's our source of strength to serve when we don't have it in us on our own. Yet availing ourselves of the Spirit's resources—taking action to love and serve people—opens us up to more of the Spirit's guiding, strengthening resources. By loving, we increase our resources for loving, and the Spirit becomes a constant presence for us.

Question 7. As we saw in session 3, serving often tires us out. And we often don't know what is the best way to serve someone or don't believe we have what it takes. All we have are a few loaves and fishes! The Holy Spirit strengthens us to do what we couldn't do alone and provides us wisdom to give people what they truly need.

Question 10. We often think that we need to choose between a life of service and a life of prayerful intimacy with Christ. While both the active and the contemplative sides of our spiritual lives are important, serving others gives us an intimacy with Christ that prayer or worship alone can't. We need both.

Question 12. Ideally, you should do this exercise on your own before the meeting and briefly share the results to show your group the possibilities. Trying it first will also help you answer their questions. Then give people five minutes of quiet to do this exercise. Afterward, allow time for them to share the results, either with the whole group or in smaller circles of three or four people.

Question 14. Again, you should be sure to do this exercise on your own and come to the next meeting ready to share what happened. You'll lead best when you model servanthood and openness.

SESSION FIVE:
BONDSLAVES

Question 3. There's no getting around the fact that slavery is a shocking way to describe our relationship with God. If you find this passage shocking, go ahead and say so. Allow others to express their negative feelings. Then let the group talk about why they think Jesus chose this imagery. The Study Notes should be helpful here.

Question 4. If some group members have strongly negative reactions, this question will give them permission to express those feelings. Many groups—African-Americans, immigrants, workers, women—have been exploited in the name of Christian servanthood. Even some churches and ministries justify substandard pay and benefits to lower-level staff by pointing to servanthood. All of that is true. Nonetheless, Jesus calls all of us—including leaders—to this same bondslave attitude. We need to immerse ourselves in the picture of God the Bible presents until we can clearly see that while God is our Master, he's a wise, loving Master who always seeks what is good for his servants. He's a far better master than any human bosses we've had. Unless we trust God to be a good Master, we'll never really relax into a servant relationship with him.

Questions 5 and 6. If we reject God, we're slaves to sin, which leads to death (Romans 6:23). This is hard for many people to accept. They're nice, hardworking people who don't have any obvious "slavery," such as an addiction. They're unaware of their slavery to pride, possessions, envy, ambition for themselves or their children, perfectionism, anger, anxiety, other people's approval, indifference to others' suffering, or simply the drive to get their own way. Even more, they're unaware of their slavery to the inevitable consequence of sin: death. They don't know that by trying to live free from God, they're shackling themselves to eternal death.

Most of what humans do is controlled by habits—habits of thinking, habitual emotional responses to events, and habits of behavior. Those who reject the Holy Spirit's work of shaping their habits of mind, feeling, and action are controlled by habits that are rooted in lies such as, "Everything depends on me" and "Look out for number one." Their desires and feelings compel them to automatic reactions and choices. They don't freely choose to lose their temper—they can't help it. They don't freely choose to lie awake worrying, and they're unable to freely choose to stop doing it. They don't freely choose to be sexually attracted to someone other than their spouse, and they may feel powerless to resist the attraction. That's slavery to sin.

The decision to become Christ's disciple sets a believer free from the fundamental orientation toward sin and from its death penalty. The ongoing work of truth (John 8:32) and the Spirit of truth in a person's life progressively drive out the lies and habits that give sin its power. The person begins by *choosing* to believe and *wanting* to obey the truth and then becomes increasingly able to choose to obey the truth.

Question 12. This could be an extremely fruitful discussion for your group. It will be important not to point fingers at any individuals, but to have a general discussion about sharing responsibilities. You may take this opportunity to affirm those who have been servants in your group—maybe behind the scenes. Spin the conversation in a positive direction. Sometimes people aren't serving because they haven't been asked, or they don't feel they have what it takes to do the job, or because they're serving hard somewhere else, or because some temporary life situation (like a baby in the house) makes it impossible for them to do more than show up at a meeting.

One final thing in this session is to confirm the group's interest in continuing to another study in this series. Show them the next study guide (*Sharing Christ Together*) and collect the money in advance, or pick up the books and have them pay you later.

Question 3. Showing hospitality to friends is good, but the deepest service is when we don't receive a reward from people. Give some thought to the ways in which your entertaining or monetary giving is self-serving.

Question 4. This question harks back to session 2, where Jesus said that service to the needy is service to Christ himself.

Questions 7 and 10. Who are the people in your church or neighborhood who live alone and have few friends? The offbeat people? The one whose life is a mess? Identify some names and see if there's a way your group could serve or offer hospitality to one or more of these people. One of you might have a neighbor with a messy life (such as someone getting off drugs or a single mother with a complicated boyfriend history), and on your own you're reluctant to get involved. But teamed up with one or more members of your group, you could invite that person over for coffee.

Question 11. You can't serve everyone constantly. But you can serve someone consistently, or a few people over the course of a week, or several people in small ways each day. Talk about your limits.

Question 12. Whether your group is ending or continuing, it's important to celebrate where you have come together. If you choose not to discuss question 1 during your meeting, it would be a great question to discuss at a party. Be sure the spiritual partner time is honored.

Thank everyone for what they've contributed to the group. You might even give some thought ahead of time to something unique each person has contributed. You can say those things at the beginning of your meeting.

ABOUT THE AUTHORS

The authors' previous work as a team includes the DOING LIFE TOGETHER Bible study series, which won a Silver Medallion from the Evangelical Christian Publishers Association, as well as the DOING LIFE TOGETHER DVD series.

Brett Eastman has served as the champion of Small Groups and Leadership Development for both Willow Creek Community Church and Saddleback Valley Community Church. Brett is now the Founder and CEO of Lifetogether, a ministry whose mission is to "transform lives through community." Brett earned his Masters of Divinity degree from Talbot School of Theology and his Management Certificate from Kellogg School of Business at Northwestern University. **Dee Eastman** is the real hero in the family, who, after giving birth to Joshua and Breanna, gave birth to identical triplets—Meagan, Melody, and Michelle. They live in Las Flores, California.

Todd and Denise Wendorff serve at King's Harbor Church in Redondo Beach, California. Todd is a teaching pastor, handles leadership development, and pastors men. He is also coauthor of the Every Man Bible Study Series. Denise speaks to women at conferences, classes, and special events. She also serves women through personal discipleship. Previously, Todd was on the pastoral staff at Harvest Bible Chapel, Willow Creek Community Church, and Saddleback Valley Community Church. He holds a Th.M. from Talbot School of Theology. Todd and Denise live in Rolling Hills Estates, California with their three children, Brooke, Brittany, and Brandon.

Karen Lee-Thorp has written or cowritten more than fifty books and Bible studies, including *How to Ask Great Questions* and *Why Beauty Matters.* Her previous Silver Medallion winners are *The Story of Stories, LifeChange: Ephesians,* and *LifeChange: Revelation.* She was a senior editor at NavPress for many years and series editor for the LifeChange Bible study series. She is now a freelance writer, speaks at women's retreats, and trains small group leaders. She lives in Brea, California, with her husband, Greg Herr, and their daughters, Megan and Marissa.

SMALL GROUP ROSTER

Name	Address	Phone	Email Address	Team or Role	Church Ministry
Bill Jones	7 Alvalar street L.F. 92665	766-2255	bjones@aol.com	socials	children's ministry

(Pass your book around your group at your first meeting to get everyone's name and contact information.)

Name	Address	Phone	Email Address	Team or Role	Church Ministry

Experiencing Christ Together:
Living with Purpose in Community

Brett & Dee Eastman; Todd & Denise Wendorff;
Karen Lee-Thorp

Experiencing Christ Together: Living with Purpose in Community is a series of six, six-week study guides that offers small groups a chance to explore Jesus' teaching on the five biblical purposes of the church. By closely examining Christ's life and teaching in the Gospels, the series helps group members walk in the steps of Christ's early followers. Jesus lived every moment following God's purposes for his life, and Experiencing Christ Together helps groups learn how they can do this too. The first book lays the foundation: who Christ is and what he has done for us. Each of the other five books in the series looks at how Jesus trained his followers to live one of the five biblical purposes (fellowship, discipleship, service, evangelism, and worship).

	Softcovers	DVD
Beginning in Christ Together	ISBN: 0-310-24986-4	ISBN: 0-310-26187-2
Connecting in Christ Together	ISBN: 0-310-24981-3	ISBN: 0-310-26189-9
Growing in Christ Together	ISBN: 0-310-24985-6	ISBN: 0-310-26192-9
Serving Like Christ Together	ISBN: 0-310-24984-8	ISBN: 0-310-26194-5
Sharing Christ Together	ISBN: 0-310-24983-X	ISBN: 0-310-26196-1
Surrendering to Christ Together	ISBN: 0-310-24982-1	ISBN: 0-310-26198-8

Pick up a copy today at your favorite bookstore!

ZONDERVAN™

GRAND RAPIDS, MICHIGAN 49530 USA

WWW.ZONDERVAN.COM

Doing Life Together series

Brett & Dee Eastman; Todd & Denise Wendorff;
Karen Lee-Thorp

Based on the five biblical purposes that form the bedrock of Saddleback Church, Doing Life Together will help your group discover what God created you for and how you can turn this dream into an everyday reality. Experience the transformation firsthand as you begin Connecting, Growing, Developing, Sharing, and Surrendering your life together for him.

"Doing Life Together is a groundbreaking study . . . [It's] the first small group curriculum built completely on the purpose-driven paradigm . . . The greatest reason I'm excited about [it] is that I've seen the dramatic changes it produces in the lives of those who study it."
—FROM THE FOREWORD BY RICK WARREN

Small Group Ministry Consultation

Building a healthy, vibrant, and growing small group ministry is challenging. That's why Brett Eastman and a team of certified coaches are offering small group ministry consultation. Join pastors and church leaders from around the country to discover new ways to launch and lead a healthy Purpose-Driven small group ministry in your church. To find out more information please call 1-800-467-1977.

	Softcover	
Beginning Life Together	ISBN: 0-310-24672-5	ISBN: 0-310-25004-8
Connecting with God's Family	ISBN: 0-310-24673-3	ISBN: 0-310-25005-6
Growing to Be Like Christ	ISBN: 0-310-24674-1	ISBN: 0-310-25006-4
Developing Your SHAPE to Serve Others	ISBN: 0-310-24675-X	ISBN: 0-310-25007-2
Sharing Your Life Mission Every Day	ISBN: 0-310-24676-8	ISBN: 0-310-25008-0
Surrendering Your Life for God's Pleasure	ISBN: 0-310-24677-6	ISBN: 0-310-25009-9
Curriculum Kit	ISBN: 0-310-25002-1	

ZONDERVAN™

GRAND RAPIDS, MICHIGAN 49530 USA

WWW.ZONDERVAN.COM

Life Together Student Edition
Brett Eastman & Doug Fields

The Life Together series is the beginning of a relational journey, from being a member of a group to being a vital part of an unbelievable spiritual community. These books will help you think, talk, dig deep, care, heal, share . . . and have the time of your life! Life . . . together!

The Life Together Student Edition DVD Curriculum combines DVD teaching from well-known youth Bible teachers, as well as leadership training, with the Life Together Student Edition Small Group Series to give a new way to do small group study and ministry with basic training on how to live healthy and balanced lives-purpose driven lives.

STARTING to Go Where God Wants You to Be-Student Edition	ISBN: 0-310-25333-0
CONNECTING Your Heart to Others'-Student Edition	ISBN: 0-310-25334-9
GROWING to Be Like Jesus-Student Edition	ISBN: 0-310-25335-7
SERVING Others in Love-Student Edition	ISBN: 0-310-25336-5
SHARING Your Story and God's Story-Student Edition	ISBN: 0-310-25337-3
SURRENDERING Your Life to Honor God-Student Edition	ISBN: 0-310-25338-1
Small Group Leader's Guide Volume 1	ISBN: 0-310-25339-x
Small Group Leader's Guide Volume 2	ISBN: 0-310-25340-3
Small Group Leader's Guide Volume 3	ISBN: 0-310-25341-1

Pick up a copy today at your favorite bookstore!

ZONDERVAN™

GRAND RAPIDS, MICHIGAN 49530 USA

WWW.ZONDERVAN.COM

life**together**.com